GOD'S FRUIT SALAD

A Divine Recipe for a filling Life

DIANA KINSER

WESTBOW
PRESS®
A DIVISION OF THOMAS NELSON
& ZONDERVAN

WestBow Press books may be ordered through booksellers or by contacting:

WestBow Press
A Division of Thomas Nelson & Zondervan
1663 Liberty Drive
Bloomington, IN 47403
www.westbowpress.com
844-714-3454

"Scripture quotations are from the ESV® Bible (The Holy Bible, English Standard Version®), copyright © 2001 by Crossway, a publishing ministry of Good News Publishers. Used by permission. All rights reserved."

Scripture quotations taken from The Holy Bible, New International Version® NIV® Copyright © 1973 1978 1984 2011 by Biblica, Inc. TM. Used by permission. All rights reserved worldwide.

Scripture quotations marked (NLT) are taken from the Holy Bible, New Living Translation, copyright ©1996, 2004, 2015 by Tyndale House Foundation. Used by permission of Tyndale House Publishers, a Division of Tyndale House Ministries, Carol Stream, Illinois 60188. All rights reserved.

Scripture taken from The Message. Copyright © 1993, 1994, 1995, 1996, 2000, 2001, 2002. Used by permission of NavPress Publishing Group.

ISBN: 978-1-6642-5672-9 (sc)
ISBN: 978-1-6642-5674-3 (hc)
ISBN: 978-1-6642-5673-6 (e)

Library of Congress Control Number: 2022901807

Print information available on the last page.

WestBow Press rev. date: 02/09/2022

Dedication

A special thank you to my family--

To my children, *Leslie Bullock and Ryan Toombs*. When you were growing up you taught me that one can't survive being a parent without a strong faith, unending patience, and a good sense of humor. Now that you are adults, you are more my friends than my children. You fill my life with so many blessings. Not only do I love you more than you can imagine, but I'm also very proud of you both.

To my husband, *Clay Kinser*. Your many words of encouragement during this writing and publishing process have given me the courage to step out in faith. This book would not have happened without your unwavering support. My heart is full of love and gratitude.

To my precious granddaughters – *Kaydence, Abigail, and Sophia* – you bring me joy and laughter and make me feel young again. To my grandson, *Maddox*, you rock! And I'm not just talking about your amazing music skills! I pray all four of you will always put the Lord first in your lives. He alone will help you when you doubt your worth. He alone will give you strength in the tough times and peace when nothing or no one else can. I love you!

And to my friends –

To my sweet friend, *Arden Thorne*. You are such an inspiration to me and hundreds of others. Even in your struggles and pain, you never give up. You model the fruit of the Spirit better than anyone I know. I am a stronger person for knowing you.

To my dear friend, *Beth Basinger*. You are more than my friend; you are my sister who has blessed my life in so many ways. Your faith and wisdom have strengthened and guided me more times than you know. I am grateful and thank God for you. Your encouragement and support in this writing process filled me with strength and courage.

And to my friend and brother, *Jeff Jenkins* – Your writing has inspired me, your words have uplifted me, your faith has challenged me, and your friendship has blessed my life. You have made me a better person and a stronger Christian in so many ways. Saying thank you is just inadequate.

Acknowledgments

Clark Hornbaker, owner and general manager of the beautiful Eden Hill Winery, Celina, TX. Thank you for allowing me to hang out and experience the fruit of your vineyard and the fruit of your wisdom. Meeting you was such a blessing. Thanks also to Sheri Richter, Eden Hill's office manager, Linda Hornbaker, Clark's lovely wife, and Chris Hornbaker, the man with the magic (also known as the winemaker). Your input has been invaluable.

WestBow Press. Thank you to my editorial and design teams. You made my dream a reality (and even better than I imagined).

than venturing out to work. TV mom June Cleaver (from *Leave It to Beaver*) was the role model for the perfect wife and mother. She always had a perfectly clean home, perfectly decorated furnishings, and perfectly prepared meals. She proudly served her family's meals on a silver tray while wearing lovely dresses, heels, and pearls, and with perfect makeup and beautifully coiffed hairstyles. She was never tired or frazzled. She never had any personal problems. She was never sad, lonely, or depressed. Life in Mayfield, USA, was ideal.

Even though it was rarely discussed, many women looked at their own lives and couldn't understand why they felt inadequate. They wanted to be June Cleaver, but life wasn't working out that way. No one really discussed self-esteem issues, depression, anxiety, and loneliness. Women were tired and unhappy but didn't know why. They thought they just needed to try harder, redecorate the house, or maybe have another baby. They felt guilty that they couldn't get it right.

To make matters worse, they couldn't discuss their feelings with their husbands or doctors because they couldn't relate or help. Women just knew that their "perfect" friends (who were also hiding their feelings of inferiority) would be shocked if they ever confessed their struggles. So, they just kept quiet and tried to do their best, feeling more and more isolated and alone.

As their frustrations grew, women would often take their anger out on their children (which increased their guilt) or comfort themselves with alcohol or tranquilizers. My own "perfect" mother told me later in life that she always felt unworthy of love and had low self-esteem. She had even contemplated suicide more than once. Here was this sweet Christian woman who was loved by everyone, but she frequently said, "If they knew the real me, they wouldn't like me." Sadly, those feelings never went away for her.

Of course, women today can be anything we want to be. But feelings of inadequacy and low self-esteem can still stop us in our tracks. Today's role models, now known as "influencers," still give us unrealistic expectations that are impossible to meet. We often try to soothe our worthless feelings by shopping, overeating, or keeping busy with one commitment after another. But then we get on social media, and once again, we don't measure up.

Thankfully, women have a special place in God's plan and in his heart. He really does want us to live joyful, Spirit-filled lives. We are uniquely made and have many jobs—mothers, caregivers, teachers, counselors, nurses, chefs, and chauffeurs. But to those responsibilities, we can add roles as business owners, supervisors, technical whizzes, and hard-working employees.

Then the world turned upside down in 2020. The pandemic caused us to modify our lifestyles and tackle new responsibilities, still trying to keep some semblance of normalcy within our families, often doing all this from home and often with masks covering our faces. These unprecedented struggles were overwhelming and caused many women to feel alone, depressed, frustrated, hopeless, and just plain tired. It's the 1950s all over again!

Can you relate? Are you one of those women who feels like she is drowning and maybe even invisible to God? Have you forgotten what his peace feels like? Maybe you have never felt his presence in the first place. What if you could take a break and just sit across the table with your grandma over a cup of coffee? She would smile and hold your hand and tell you everything was going to be okay. Grandmas have a gentle way of making us feel loved and accepted.

That's just what I want you to feel when you read this book—that someone cares and wants what is best for you. Just like any other loving grandma, I wish I could take away every struggle you face. But I can tell you from many years of hard experience that the sweetest fruit in a Christian's life comes from the deepest pain.

You see, God has a fruit salad recipe for you, and he's given you the Holy Spirit to mix it all together in your life. When you let the Spirit direct your steps, his fruit of love, joy, peace, patience, kindness, goodness, faithfulness, and even self-control will become a part of who you are and who you can become. It's not an easy path, but you don't have to do it on your own. And boy am I thankful about that!

Dear Father,
I thank you that my new "granddaughter" and friend has picked up this book. Please fill her with your peace and let her know beyond a doubt how loved and precious she is to you.

May she find strength, wisdom, and growth in these pages. Thank you for your patience with us as we stumble every day. And thank you most of all for your gift of grace that Jesus gave us on the cross, making us daughters of the King!

Amen.

Chapter 1

THE POTLUCK

When I was growing up, one of my favorite activities was our church potluck. I grew up in a small town in Virginia. Even though it was a country church, our quarterly potlucks were epic. They were held on the grounds under big elm trees behind the church building. The older ladies at church were very serious about this event. Some of the stronger men put several long tables together, end to end, and the ladies carefully covered them with white tablecloths just for all the food. Smaller folding tables and chairs were scattered around for the adults, and the kids were expected to sit on a curb or under a tree. We never complained!

Everyone had to have their covered dishes in the church kitchen before Bible class. You couldn't be late! The ladies puttered around the kitchen carrying what seemed like hundreds of white Corningware casseroles, steaming Crockpots of chicken and dumplings or pot roast, a rainbow of Tupperware bowls in every size, and many foil-covered thirteen-by-nine pans filled with everything from apple cobbler to brownies to chicken and rice dishes.

It was like an orchestrated dance in that kitchen, and we kids knew to stay out of the way! The ladies made sure every cake and pie was sliced and that every casserole had a serving spoon placed in it. They artistically laid out all the main dishes first, followed by assorted vegetables (mostly all kinds of green bean dishes, cheesy "funeral" potatoes, and buttered corn). Next came the many colorful salads, and finally the rolls and condiments, including our preacher's pickled jalapeños (which I was never brave enough to try).

think, *Why did I do that again?* Many of my choices are certainly not ones you would expect from a "wise" old grandma.

But I have learned a thing or two over the years. I have realized that I don't have it within me to always do the right thing. My own selfish wants, my pride, and my thoughtlessness always get in the way. Basically, *I* get in the way. I know it sounds hopeless, but it really isn't. You see, when I allow the Holy Spirit to fill my life with his fruit, supernatural things happen! I am kinder, more loving, and more patient. I even have more self-control (which is pretty difficult at any age).

I am amazed and very grateful that God is so patient with me. He sees me struggling to mix all these ingredients together. I have the love, I add the joy, and then, oops, someone makes a U-turn in front of my car, and I forget my patience. There goes my gentleness. All the time, God is patiently waiting for me to get it right. Have you ever felt that same kind of frustration? You want to do the right thing, make godly choices, and then *you* get in your own way. He knows that the best way to grow healthy fruit in our lives is with practice, so he gives us lessons to teach us how to do so. That isn't always easy for us; sometimes it's very painful. But he knows that the outcome will be sweeter fruit. So those lessons, trials, or challenges are necessary and beneficial.

I've figured out the reason why I don't get it right. That Galatians passage does not say, "The fruit of Diana is love, peace, patience;" it says, "The fruit of the Spirit." I try too hard to do this on my own. Boy, is that tough! It just does not work. But when I ask the Spirit to lead me, love and joy come naturally. Faithfulness and gentleness are visible. I am kinder and more sensitive to others. I have more self-control and even more patience.

I know it sounds easy: Just turn your life over to the leading of the Spirit, and you will be the perfect Christian. Believe it or not, that actually is God's plan. Thankfully, he knows I am human. I mess up, and I forget that "turning over" part.

Honestly, sometimes I really don't forget, but I just don't want to let him be in charge. I have to keep reminding myself that he is on the throne, not me! Thankfully, he keeps giving me chance after chance. His mercies are new every morning, so I get to try again today and again tomorrow and every day after that.

But we want it easy, and we want it right now, don't we? We just don't have time for one more thing on our plates. After all, we are busy women with hectic schedules—kids' sports, dance lessons, gymnastics, school programs, and PTA. That doesn't include our husbands, our jobs, and our church activities. We *need* this Spirit-filled life to be easy. *Please just give it to me now, Lord!* We are so much like our children are when we are going on vacation. They are so excited about the destination at the end of the trip that all along the way, they keep asking, "Are we there yet?"

Being filled with the Spirit is a growth process. We receive the gift of the Holy Spirit, the indwelling of God himself living inside us, when we put on Christ in baptism. "Repent and be baptized every one of you in the name of Jesus Christ for the forgiveness of your sins, and you will receive the gift of the Holy Spirit" (Acts 2:38, ESV). Understanding how the Spirit works, however, comes with maturity. Actually, just like our understanding of God, we can never fully understand who the Spirit is, either. Allowing him to work in our lives and take control is even more difficult, but that is God's plan for us.

We smile when we see a toddler trying to walk around in his daddy's boots. He stumbles and falls but keeps getting up. We know that someday that little one will grow up, fill those boots, and walk confidently. That is the way the Spirit operates, too. He is there inside us, leading us, interceding for us in ways we cannot comprehend. He is there "full strength" right from the beginning, but only as we mature do we grow and make use of his power. Most of the time, there is some pain involved in this process! That pain comes from our loving Father pruning and shaping us to be more like him.

Trimming and cutting away at an apple tree is necessary for it to bear the most fruit. That pruning gives us a bountiful harvest of apples that are juicy, sweet, and delicious to eat. Just like that tree, our Father knows what is best for us. He "trims" us to allow us to bear more fruit. When we want to grow the fruit of the Spirit in our lives, then challenges and struggles will be a part of that growth. He knows how difficult and painful it can be, so he is patient with us as we face those trials. He just keeps on loving us. He smiles at us as we fall down again and again. He helps us up and cheers us on as we take one more step closer to him.

Here's the kicker—we don't have to just grit our teeth when things are tough, we can be content and, like the apostle Paul, even rejoice in our struggles! Why? Because when we are weak, then we are strong (2 Corinthians 12:10, ESV). That doesn't seem to make sense, does it? But our human weaknesses give us his supernatural strength. So, if we keep looking in his direction, it will get easier, and we will grow more and more like him.

The most important thing to understand about God's fruit salad is that it is not just for us to consume and enjoy for ourselves. He has a greater plan to use his fruit living in us to draw others to him. That has always been his plan even before he created us. The world is full of hungry people—hungry for acceptance, for peace, for love. God wants them to taste of his fruit when they see it growing and glowing in our lives. He loves every person and wants them to know it. You and I are his instruments to do that. Our divine purpose is to reflect God's love, patience, peace, and other traits that everyone is looking for. This world gives them only false and temporary solutions. They have been beaten down and discouraged. They are afraid to even hope that there could be something better and more satisfying than what they have right now. They need a Savior. As we model the fruit of the Spirit in our lives, they will see a genuine difference that they will want in their lives, too.

Before Jesus returned to heaven after his resurrection, he knew his disciples would feel lost, lonely, confused, fearful, overwhelmed, and doubtful (sound familiar?). He did not want to leave them defenseless, so he gave them a gift, the essence of God himself living inside them. He said, "And I will pray to the Father, and he will give you another Helper (or Comforter), to be with you forever" (John 14:16, ESV).

When my dad died unexpectedly a few years ago, it was probably the most challenging time in my life at that point. At the funeral service, there were hundreds of people there who loved my dad and cared about our family. They all tried to comfort us in their own unique ways. They had many words of wisdom. They quoted lots of scripture. They gave us hugs and lots of food. To be honest, I appreciated their efforts, but it really did not help to assuage my grief. What comforted me most was having my sister beside me. She was going through the same feelings as I was and fully understood the depth of our loss. We drew upon each other's strength. It was bigger than both of us. God reached down and comforted us by helping us to comfort each other.

So, when Jesus left his disciples his comforter, he knew what he was doing. He put that comforter inside each of them, to become a part of their deepest longings, their very thoughts. Jesus was giving them a part of himself. He was there when Paul was shipwrecked, when Peter first met the Gentiles, and when each of his followers struggled through persecution, fear, and even death. We have that same comforter inside us, too. He fully understands every struggle we go through.

Now that I am a "mature" Christian, at least in age, I see this Spirit-helper in new ways. He directs my steps. He lightens my burdens. He gives me hope when everyone tells me things are hopeless. The more I experience his leading, the more I ask him to lead. I learn to call upon the Spirit more and more. When I face challenges and trials, I know he will give me the strength to meet them head-on. How do I know this? Because he has already done so time and time again.

As I keep opening my heart and my will to the Spirit's guidance, then the fruit of the Spirit grows more evident in my life. I realize that the Spirit gives me that extra bit of willpower when I have no self-control of my own. When I feel angry or stressed, the Spirit gives me peace and love. He does not force it down my throat. I must ask for his help, and he eagerly gives it to me.

Honestly, the hardest part for me is to slow down long enough to recognize the Spirit working and to make use of the resources he has available to me. I see a situation and I react. I want to just jump in and take over, solve the problem, and move on. But as I continue to grow more in Christ's image and become more filled with his Spirit, this process gets easier. He reminds me to slow down. I realize that it makes more sense to be faithful because of what he had done for me in the past.

God was specific about the fruit of the Spirit—these attributes of a life in tune to his will. I don't think it was an accident that three of them focus on our relationships with others (patience, kindness, and goodness), three of them are direct demonstrations of our relationship with God (faithfulness, joy, and love), and three are aspects of our own spiritual growth (gentleness, peace, and self-control). Together, they make up our whole beings.

Think about the ramifications of this—that God, the Father himself, is allowing us to share in a part of his divine nature. His Holy Spirit gives us these nine divine qualities right up into our souls and personalities. That is amazing! The fruit of the Spirit develops in us so we can show God's nature to the world around us.

My prayer for you as you read this book is that you will learn more about the fruit of a faithful Christian life, and you will want your life to grow more into his image. I pray you will understand and appreciate how the Holy Spirit is working to help you, comfort you, and draw you closer to your Father.

By the way, you don't have to wait until you are my age to see the benefits and growth that come from a Spirit-filled life. So, as you continue to seek his will for your life, the fruit of the Spirit will mature you in ways you cannot even comprehend. Remember, you cannot do these things by your own power. You can't just say, "I'm going to go and be more loving." It is with divine power beyond our understanding that this happens. We will talk more about the Holy Spirit's power in the next chapter.

So, are you ready? It's time for a heavenly feast. We just need to allow God to pile up our plates with love, joy, peace, patience, kindness, goodness, faithfulness, gentleness, and self-control. They give our lives meaning and just the right sweetness. I guarantee it will be a salad so filling there will not be room for dessert!

> *Grandma D.'s wisdom: I hope you can remember, my dear one, that life is not about us. It's always about our Father. It's like that old hymn, "Let Him Have His Way With Thee." I promise your life will make more sense. And all that yummy fruit? I guarantee it will make your life more sweet and satisfying!*
>
> *Love, Grandma D.*

Chapter 2

NOT BY MIGHT,
NOT BY POWER

I have a confession to make. It's embarrassing, but sadly true. I started writing this book back in 1993. What? That's right. Out of the blue, the idea came into my head to write a book. I don't know why; it just did. First, I wondered what I should write about. I always loved creative writing, so I decided I should write a "best-selling" novel. I applaud those talented souls who can write such eloquent fiction that the reader can't put the book down until the final page.

Yes, that was what I was going to do. I was going to write an epic novel that everyone would want to read. No one would skip a single word; they would read it from cover to cover. I knew I would be famous and go on book tours and make lots of money. I spent so much time preparing to write and imagining the accolades I would receive when my book hit the bestseller list that I could never really get much of the story on paper. So then I tried focusing on describing who the characters would be, what they looked like, what they thought about, and their likes and dislikes. Their images filled my mind; I could see them perfectly. That boosted my confidence, but when I tried to put them on paper, they just sat there staring at me. It was a frustrating project that went nowhere. My dreams of fame and fortune went out the window. I still have the first two chapters of that book saved on my computer. I imagine it will never see a publisher's desk.

After I put that novel idea aside, I decided to write a Christian book instead. Out of the blue, I decided it should be about the fruit of the Spirit. I didn't have a clue about the Holy Spirit, but I thought I could figure it out along the way. Silly me! I was a young mother, a full-time teacher with two energetic kids, and a husband who had major health issues. But I just knew others could learn from my "wisdom."

So I began by writing the introductory chapter, filling it with fluffy, funny stories about my family. Tackling the heart of this subject, however, was not as easy. I randomly picked one fruit to write about— peace. I came up with a clever title for the chapter and wrote a few paragraphs. Again, I had funny stories, but that was about all I could come up with. Sadly, I was just "winging it." I never spent any time in Bible study or prayer. I was just writing from what I thought was my "expertise," (which honestly wasn't much).

Then life took a serious turn, and my husband had the first of two brain surgeries for epilepsy. It was a chaotic, scary time. Bill's seizures were out of control even after doctors had tried every medication available. We hoped and prayed that the surgery would finally take away his seizures, and that we could have a normal life. I set the book aside, not even realizing that our family's struggles were teaching me the very thing I was trying to write about—peace.

A few years went by, and the book was forgotten. Then one day, about twelve years later, I came across that book file on my computer. I skimmed through what I had written, and I decided it was a good time to finish it. Now, you would think after all those years that I had learned some valuable lessons about the fruit of the Spirit in my own life. In the time between my first attempt and the second one, my dad died unexpectedly, my mom had cancer, and my husband had a second brain surgery. His seizures were causing him to be violent, and I had suffered both physically and emotionally.

I'm not saying that God was not with us during all these trials. Oh, he was! I am so grateful for his presence. At times, it was all I could do just to hang on. However, I still wrote what I thought were sweet-sounding words that would make people think, *Wow, she sure is a good writer, and so wise, too!* It was still about me; I didn't write what was necessarily true or beneficial, and I certainly didn't connect the message with my life. I had experiences that others could have related to, but again, it was all about what sounded good. I remember one platitude that still makes me cringe: "Peace is not the absence of conflict, but the ability to cope with it." That sounds like something you would find on a refrigerator magnet, but honestly, how helpful would that be to anyone?

I had two chapters written and had started writing one on faithfulness, but I just couldn't do it. I hit a wall. Nothing sounded right. I still could not see the connection between real life and the book, even though the Holy Spirit kept trying to get my attention. Once again, life got in the way, and I set the book aside. I just knew that would be the end of it.

Bill had a second brain surgery that was also unsuccessful, and his personality changed. The conflicts, anger, and violence in our home were difficult to manage. At other times, he would withdraw and not speak to anyone for days and days.

On May 26, 2006, as I was heading out for the last day of school, Bill had another severe seizure, but this time he suffocated in bed. Life took another unexpected turn. There were now new paths for me to navigate—being a widow and a single parent.

Many other challenging events also occurred through the years. I always knew God was working in my life. I felt his presence and knew my "lean-ability" was making me stronger and more faithful to him. But it never occurred to me that those trials were pruning me to be used for God's purpose. I'm sure God was probably shaking his head, wondering if I would ever learn!

Fast forward another fourteen years to 2020. My life was filled with so many blessings. I was happily married again. I had a grandson and three granddaughters, including the cutest three-year-old twin girls. I was part of a loving church family. All was good.

Then in April, I felt terrible. I went to the doctor and found out I had contracted COVID-19 and pneumonia. I was very sick and was admitted to ICU where I was put on a breathing machine for two weeks. My husband, Clay, could only drop me off at the ER door. He could not go into the hospital or even visit me at all for those two weeks. Since the COVID epidemic was still in the early days, the hospital staff was nervous to be around me. It felt like I had the plague, which I guess I did! It was scary and lonely.

Even though I was still very weak, I thankfully recovered enough to be released from the hospital. I stayed isolated at home for weeks and months just to regain my strength and to overcome long-lasting side effects. I was so grateful to be alive. But, for the first time in many years, I questioned my purpose. Actually, I was trying to figure out what God wanted me to do with my life. After all, he was the reason I had survived when so many others had not. That is surely not a typical question you ask yourself when you are a retired grandmother! But I prayed earnestly that God would show me what to do. Then, for the first time in a very long time, I thought about that book. The thought kind of just popped into my head—this time from a completely different perspective. What does all of that have to do with the Holy Spirit? Everything! I'll explain in a minute.

As hard as we try to understand how the Holy Spirit works in our lives, it is not something we can easily do. Our human minds just cannot comprehend how he works and what he does. That is because the Holy Spirit is God. God is not like us. He is holy, and therefore it is impossible to fully understand who he is. He doesn't tell us everything about himself. God only shows us little glimpses of himself, but mostly he is a mystery. He gives us clues into his nature, but he knows we really are incapable of understanding his greatness. He is the one and only God, mighty, and unfathomable. In Deuteronomy 29:29 (ESV), it says, "The secret things belong to the Lord our God, but the things revealed belong to us and to our children forever, that we may follow all the words of this law." Someday we will understand fully who he is, and then we will fall down to worship him at his throne. First Corinthians 13:12 (ESV) tells us, "For now we see in a mirror dimly, but then face to face; then I shall know fully, even as I have been fully known!" Won't that be amazing?

Now, trying to understand this trinity concept—God the Father, God the Son, and God the Holy Spirit—is just impossible for our little human minds to fully grasp. God is three in one? God is one? Many scholarly people have tried to explain how this can be, but honestly, they are just superficial. Thankfully, he doesn't expect us to understand.

Jesus and God are one. God and the Holy Spirit are one. Jesus and the Holy Spirit are one. But they are also unique personalities with unique purposes. Jesus is God who came to earth in human form as a man. He lived like us but was perfect in every way and was without sin. He did many miraculous things to show us how much God loves us. He was fully God and fully man. That is another one of those hard-to-grasp concepts, isn't it?

His followers never understood it either. Jesus had so much patience with them. In John 14, they had so many questions for him. *Where are you going? Can we go with you? How do we get there?* Then Philip told Jesus, "Lord, just show us the Father, and that will be enough for us" (John 14:8, ESV). Jesus just shook his head and said, "Oh, Philip, have I been with you for so long, and you still don't know me?" He was telling them that he and the Father are one. "Do you not yet believe that I am in the Father and the Father is in me?" (John 14:10).

Even though there is so much about God that we do not know, we still know enough to give him all our worship and praise. He calls us his children and loves us with a supernatural love beyond what we can grasp. Think about it—this all-powerful God, who created everything and everyone, sent himself to die for us so we can be forgiven and live with him forever. Then, when we accept his gift and are baptized for the forgiveness of our sins, he comes inside us, to fill us with his divine power and strength (Acts 2:38). We become the holy temple of God with his Spirit living in us.

In the Old Testament, the temple was an important place. It was where the children of Israel would go to worship God. God dwelled in the temple. Many times, the Israelites forgot about God, and his temple would fall into disrepair or be destroyed. Their lives were in shambles as well because they had forgotten their first love. Then when the New Testament opened, Jesus called himself the temple. "Destroy this temple and in three days I will raise it up again" (John 2:19, ESV). Of course, none of the Jewish leaders or even Jesus's followers had any clue that he was talking about himself and his resurrection.

After Jesus went back to heaven, the Holy Spirit moved into the lives of believers. Now, we, too, are called God's temple, because his Spirit lives and dwells in us just as he did in the man-made temple long ago. "Do you not know that you are God's temple and that God's Spirit dwells in you?" (1 Corinthians 3:16, ESV). "Or do you not know that your body is a temple of the Holy Spirit within you, whom you have from God? You are not your own, for you were bought with a price. So glorify God in your body" (1 Corinthians 6:19–20, ESV).

We have to remember that the Holy Spirit is not an "it." He is a person to be followed, not a supernatural, mindless force with powers like Superman. He wasn't just some afterthought. Just like God, he has been around since before the beginning of time.

The Holy Spirit was there at creation! In Genesis 1:2 (ESV), it says, "And the Spirit of God was hovering over the waters." A little later, when it was time to create humanity, God said, "Let *us* make man in *our* image, after *our* likeness" (Genesis 1:26, ESV). God wasn't just talking to himself. All three of them—God, Jesus, and the Holy Spirit—were there at that important moment.

The Holy Spirit was very active throughout the Old Testament. He empowered the prophets to speak the words of God and to tell of the coming Messiah. He guided the priests to intercede for God's people. He empowered the kings to lead Israel into battle against their enemies. Even during those four hundred tumultuous years between the Old Testament and the beginning of the New Testament, the Holy Spirit was not sleeping. God's wayward children were feeling more and more hopeless. The Holy Spirit was preparing the stage for their salvation and ours—the birth of a baby in Bethlehem—Jesus Christ the Lord!

The Spirit was there when Mary conceived that baby and when Jesus took his first human breath. He celebrated with those poor dirty shepherds while they joyfully danced as a heavenly choir serenaded them and their smelly sheep. He was there in the temple with Jesus and the priests while Jesus's parents frantically searched everywhere for him. He knew, more than that young boy could yet understand, what his mission was going to be. I can imagine it was a moment that was both proud and painful to him.

The Holy Spirit expressed godly joy when John baptized Jesus in the wilderness. "As soon as Jesus was baptized, he went up out of the water. At that moment heaven was opened, and he saw the Spirit of God descending like a dove and alighting on him. And a voice from heaven said, 'This is my Son, whom I love; with him I am well pleased'" (Matthew 3:16–17, NIV).

The same Holy Spirit stayed with our Savior in the wilderness and gave him strength when he was tempted by Satan. He was with Jesus struggling and praying in the garden of Gethsemane. He was always there with Jesus throughout his life. I imagine the Spirit continually gave him strength and courage, peace, and hope, always reminding him of his Father waiting for him back home. That's why Jesus referred to the Spirit as his helper and comforter.

Because the Spirit was such an important part of Jesus's own life, he wanted to share that with his disciples. On the night before his crucifixion, Jesus told his disciples that even though he would not be with them physically anymore, they would never be alone. In fact, in John 16:7 (ESV), Jesus told them, "It's to your advantage that I go away. Because if I do not go away, then the Helper will not come to you." Can you imagine that? They had been with him for three years, walking alongside him, talking, and laughing together every day. They saw him calm the sea, walk on water, feed thousands, heal the sick, raise the dead, and love the unlovable. How could anything be better than that? But Jesus loved them too much to let them fend for themselves. He knew that they would be facing tough times, persecution, pain, and even death for his sake. So, he promised to give them a comforter, a part of himself. This helper would not just be with them, but he would be *in* them forever. That meant they would never be alone. He would strengthen and guide them, as well as give them power and wisdom.

As I mentioned previously, truly understanding who the Holy Spirit is can be beyond what our tiny brains can fathom. But what he does for us is obvious and can bring so much fulfillment to our lives. He comforts us, teaches us how to understand the scriptures, guides us to make right choices, enables us to serve others, and gives us eternal life, just to name a few.

Most importantly, the Holy Spirit lives inside of us. You don't feel any difference physically with him living inside you. He's not a little flutter or a tickle in your stomach (or, for you moms, not like that first kick you felt when you were pregnant). There is none of that. But you do know the difference in your heart. He makes life better and fuller as we allow him to fill our hearts with his fruit of love, joy, peace, patience, kindness, goodness, faithfulness, gentleness, and self-control.

He becomes one with us, loving us, encouraging us, and wanting more than anything for us to yield to him every day. He truly makes life better!

One of my favorite gifts from the Spirit is that he intercedes for me when I pray. I don't know about you, but sometimes it is just so hard to find the words I want to say when I'm praying. When I am hurting, I feel so many emotions that I can't stop sobbing, and the words won't come. But the Spirit knows, and he tells the Father what I am trying to say. Sometimes, I want to ask for things that the Spirit knows are not a good idea. Other times, I forget that God is God, and I am not. I expect him to give me whatever it is I want. The Spirit intercepts my mess and sends sanctified prayers to the Father on my behalf. "In the same way, the Spirit helps us in our weakness. We do not know what we ought to pray for, but the Spirit himself intercedes for us with wordless groans. And he who searches our hearts knows the mind of the Spirit, because the Spirit intercedes for God's people according to the will of God" (Romans 8:26–27, NIV).

So, I bet you were wondering if I would ever explain how this book came to be. Well, it took me a long time to realize that the Holy Spirit has always been with me, weaving the tapestry of my life. I now understand that he has been using all the events in my life—both good and bad—to draw me closer to him. It took almost dying to finally get my attention. He has been so, so patient with me over the years. He knew back in 1993 that he would finally have his way, and I would yield to his power all these years later. It took many painful lessons because I was a slow learner, but oh how much I appreciate every one of them. Because he fills me, guides me, and loves me, I want to be everything he wants me to be. You see, once the Spirit of God is living in you and guiding your steps, you don't want to live any other way. Earlier in Romans 8:5–6, the apostle Paul wrote, "But those who live according to the Spirit, set their minds on the things of the Spirit. For to set the mind on the flesh is death, but to set the mind on the Spirit is life and peace." All I can say to that is, amen!

As I reread the chapters I wrote all those years ago, it made me feel a bit sad that I never figured it out back then. It seems like I wasted so much time! But I know now that I wasn't ready to figure it out.

God's timing is perfect. I finally understand; it is not about me. I was determined to rewrite this book from a godly perspective. I eagerly asked the Holy Spirit to make me get out of his way, so these words would be his rather than mine. That required praying every day, as well as editing, rewriting, erasing, and pruning, not just the words, but my heart.

Honestly, this long process has made my prayer life more in tune with the Spirit than ever before. This book wasn't ready in 1993 or in 2006. It amazes me that God knew that all along. He just kept being patient with me until I was ready to let him have his way. I am far from perfect! I still have so much I need to learn, but I am becoming. I am becoming transformed into his image a little more every day. It's a lifelong process, but a joyful one.

As we seek to yield our lives to the Holy Spirit, he gives us sweet fruit to make our lives better—fruit we can share with others that will do the same for them. Love, joy, peace, patience, kindness, goodness, faithfulness, gentleness, and self-control—don't they sound delicious?

> *Grandma D.'s wisdom: It's not always easy to trust that the Lord knows what is best for you. So I encourage you to follow that famous sports slogan—"Just do it!" Don't wait as long as I did. You might be missing out on some supernatural power in your life!*
>
> *Love, Grandma D.*

Chapter 3

LOVE. PERIOD.

We've all heard the saying, *We saved the best for last.* Well, God had it backward. When he told Paul to share with us about the fruit of the Holy Spirit, He started with the best—love! You see, God is excited about love! It isn't just what he does; it's who he is! God is love—pure, selfless, all-encompassing, unconditional, creative, adoring love. It is so marvelous and *big* that we can never understand all of it! It is by learning to love that we will reflect all the other fruit of the Holy Spirit living in us.

In Ephesians 3:16–19 (ESV), Paul prayed, "According to the riches of His glory, may he grant you to be strengthened with power through his Spirit in your inner being, so that Christ may dwell in your hearts through faith—that you, being rooted and grounded in love, may have strength to comprehend with all the saints how wide, how long, how high, and how deep his love is, and to know the love of Christ that surpasses understanding, that you may be filled with the fullness of God." I like the way the New Living Translation says it in verse nineteen: "May you experience the love of Christ, though it is *too great* to understand fully." Isn't that the truth!

We could write books and books just about God's love for us. It really is something greater than our human minds can understand, but his love is always true and dependable—and the best part is that it is never-failing. It's just like the relationship between a husband and wife should be.

When a couple plans their wedding, they think about all the

details—the venue, the cake, the flowers, the music, the dress, the photographer, and so much more. They are excited and can hardly wait for the big day to arrive. The most important part of that special day, however, is the ceremony itself. This is because the ceremony is a precious covenant, a binding promise, between this man and woman and God.

Sadly, nowadays, many Christian couples don't believe that the words "until death do us part" apply to them. Or maybe they forget. A husband hurts his wife's feelings (it could be something small or something big and cruel). She feels resentment and pain. She may get angry or pull away. If they don't resolve the conflict right away, the negative feelings grow into bitterness and withdrawal of love. Then she may rationalize that *God wouldn't want me to be unhappy, would he?* The divorce rate for Christian marriages is almost as high as the rest of the world! A couple must keep God at the center of their relationship and always make their spouse a godly priority. When asked how they stayed married for seventy years, an elderly gentleman smiled and said, "I always hold her hand. And I always tell her she's right."

A covenant in marriage is such a beautiful thing in God's eyes. In fact, throughout scripture, he refers to us as his bride. That is why from the beginning of time, he has made a covenant with us. The basis of God's covenant with us is his immeasurable love; it is not a feeling at all. Love is his whole being and character. He yearns for us to show him our love in return, but his love is not based on our responses. He can never be anything but love.

If you think about it, when God created the world, he could have done things so much differently. He could have commanded all men to bow down, to show him great respect, and to honor him as the "almighty God, creator of heaven and earth" (said in a loud booming voice with lots of lightning and thunder). That would have required our actions, maybe even responses in fear, but not our hearts.

But God had a completely different idea. He always wanted a personal relationship with us, to be our Father, and to love us and bless us. Ephesians 1:4 (NIV) says, "He chose us in him before the creation of the world ..." You see, God did not just create Adam and Eve, he *chose us*, too. He made a covenant with humanity before he ever created the world. He wants us to *want* to love him, and he gives us free will to do so or not. We had no part in making the conditions or terms of that covenant, but it isn't complicated or impossible to keep. Just as in a marriage, a covenant is a promise in a relationship, one that both parties agree to and honor because they are committed to each other in love. There are blessings that come if the relationship is kept, and there are penalties that come if the relationship is broken.

What is God's stipulation? He wants us to love him back. An expert of the law asked Jesus, *"Which is the greatest commandment in the law?"* Jesus replied, "Love the Lord your God with all your heart, with all your soul, and with all your mind. This is *the first and greatest commandment."* Jesus further said, "And the second is like it: Love your neighbor as yourself" (Matthew 22:36–39, NIV).

So, there are just two things God expects of us—love God and love people. That's it! Love God with all your heart, soul, and strength. And love people the same way. Love. Period. That may sound simplistic— just love God and love people. There is no "just" about it! When you love with all your heart, soul, and strength, you will want to please him with everything you do. We can never match God's perfect love, but as we grow in our love for him and for others, then we are being transformed more and more into his image. We become more like him in every aspect of our lives.

God's love is unrivaled in all of history. Even the greatest love stories of all time cannot hold a candle to his love for us! And to prove his love for us even more, God did something so unbelievable that it brings me to tears. What did he do? He sent his only son Jesus to become a human being like us, not as a full-grown man, but as a helpless newborn baby. He grew up without sin, and he showed the world what his Father is like. He did that by loving, serving, teaching, guiding, and drawing us to him. He knew our hunger for peace and our thirst for living water. And he wanted all of us to be satisfied. He demonstrated how to love and care for others. He healed the sick, the blind, the lame, the weak, and the deaf. He forgave those the world saw as worthless and unforgivable (like me!).

If that had been all Jesus did, it would have been more than enough. But, believe it or not, he did even more; he did the unthinkable. He willingly chose to die a horrible death on a cross, taking all our sins on his shoulders—my sins, your sins, and the sins of everyone from the beginning until the end of time! This perfect Lamb took away the sins of the world. He washed me clean, and I'll never be dirty again! He washed you, too, so you would never feel worthless, ugly, or invisible, or ever again doubt how much you are loved.

There isn't anything greater our Father could do for us to show us his love. Because of Jesus's death, God has offered us his mercy and grace. Mercy means he doesn't give us what we deserve (e.g., eternal punishment). But he also gives us grace, which means he forgives us and promises us a home with him in heaven. We don't deserve that, either.

Want to hear something else that is pretty awesome? He knows that we mess up every day, and he keeps on forgiving us and loving us! Unbelievable, isn't it? He never would tell you that he's done forgiving you because you've messed up one time too many. Sometimes we think that might be true, but it's not. Sometimes it's hard to forgive ourselves, isn't it? But that's not what he does. His is such an amazing kind of love; he is passionate about you and me! He washes us clean every morning! "The steadfast love of the Lord *never* ceases; his mercies *never* come to an end; they are new every morning; great is your faithfulness" (Lamentations 3:22–23, ESV). Why would we ever want to walk away from him? Let's look further at some traits of God's love. After all, he wants us to love others the way he does. That can be pretty overwhelming. Let's look at just how wonderful his love is.

God's love is unconditional. He loves you and he loves me in spite of ourselves. He sees the mistakes that we repeat again and again, and he does not quit. He never turns his back on us. He never walks away. He says, "Fear not, for I have redeemed you; I have called you by name, you are mine!" (Isaiah 43:1, ESV). He is in the stands cheering the loudest for us. He knows our worst thoughts, our worst choices, and our biggest mistakes, and he never leaves! Think about that. Even before he created you, he knew all the things you would do in this life. He knew your highest highs and your lowest lows. He knew your tears before they wet your eyes. He knew those times you wanted to quit. He was there when you were sad, lonely, and disappointed. He knows your heart right now! Nothing you do is ever a surprise to him. You were on his mind when he created the world. You were on his mind when he allowed the nails to pierce his hands. You were on his heart when he breathed his last breath.

God's love is never-ending. His death, you see, was his beautiful plan to allow you to live with him forever. He claims you as his own child, not a hired servant, not the cook or the maid, not some poor, penniless distant relative. You are royalty! You will live in his palace, feast at his table, and live in the presence of his love for all eternity. Yes, God's love truly goes on and on; it is never-ending. "For I am sure that neither death nor life, nor angels nor rulers, nor things present nor things to come, nor powers, nor height nor depth, nor anything else in all creation, will be able to separate us from the love of God in Christ Jesus our Lord" (Romans 8:38–39, ESV). Absolutely nothing can pull you from his loving arms!

God's love is patient. He not only knows your thoughts and your dreams; he knows your future as well. He is already there. He loves you no matter what you do tomorrow or even ten or twenty years from now. When you cry, *Why, Lord?* I imagine he just shakes his head. He wishes you could just be patient. He is still right there beside you, hoping you will trust him. You see, he knows that the tapestry of your life is still being woven and that everything will work out for your good. Even if you give up on yourself, he is there. Even when you give up on him, he is patiently waiting for you with open arms. He knows every choice you will ever make, and it does not change how he feels about you now and forever. Think about that—the creator of the universe chose you to be his child. Someone once said, "If God had a refrigerator, your picture would be on it!"

God's love is perfect. As hard as we try, we can never love as God loves us. He loves every person in this world even when they couldn't care less about him. "He makes his sun rise on the evil and on the good, and he sends rain on the just and on the unjust" (Matthew 5:45, ESV). Everyone has felt God's love in some way, even if they never acknowledge him. God's love does not rely on how much we love him. He will not love you more if you love him more. He will not love you less, either. Because he *is* love, he loves you perfectly all the time in every way. His promise to us is the same promise he told his children long ago: "I have loved you with an everlasting love; I have drawn you with unfailing kindness" (Jeremiah 31:3, NIV). Moses told the children of Israel what God says to us: "It was not because you were more in number than any other people that the Lord set his love on you and chose you, for you were the fewest of all peoples, but it is simply because the Lord loves you ..." (Deuteronomy 7:7–8, ESV). You, too, are chosen. You are loved.

So, how do we respond to his love? You may wonder, *how can I learn to love when I've never had real love before?* Or maybe you are suspicious of his love because you have been let down too many times. You and I both know that it is hard to give love when you don't feel it, when you feel unloved yourself. Do you look in the mirror and doubt your worth? Have you been fed negative messages from your family? *You're not smart enough. You're not good enough. You don't matter.* Do you wonder if you will ever feel the happiness of being accepted just as you are? Has your spouse rejected you? Has someone made you feel insignificant, or even worse, invisible? What messages do you tell yourself? *I am ugly. I am dumb. I cannot do anything right. I really don't matter to anyone.*

God wants you to know that all of those are *lies*! He sees your beauty; he knows your worth. Remember, he valued you enough to die for you just so he could have you with him always. That is a pretty expensive price tag on your life! He yearns for you to see yourself as he sees you. He wants you to look in that mirror, raise your arms in the air, smile, and shout, "Ta-da! I am perfect—just the way he made me to be." Yes, you are—perfect and loved.

Can you tell I'm excited about God's love for us? I know I mentioned this before, but I want you to stop and let it soak in—even before time began and he created the universe, you were in his thoughts and in his heart. Just stop here a few minutes and go read Psalm 139. It is my very favorite chapter in the Bible. I cry when I read it because it is so amazing that he made me just the way I am, fearfully and wonderfully. Seriously, go read it right now. I'll wait. (It's printed in the back of this book if you don't have your Bible handy).

When we talk about loving others, we find that *love* is not really an easy word to understand. I mean, I love pizza. I love coffee in the morning. I love my husband. I love my puppies. I love my children, and I especially adore my grandchildren! It can be confusing to know the difference in all those "loves." In ancient times, however, the Greeks were not confused because they had several different words for love! Let's look at them and see if we can determine what kind of love God has for us and what kind he wants us to have for others.

One word we translate as love is *phileo*, which means "to have a special interest in someone or something." It is friendship love. Of course, we see how *phileo* is translated as love because, in modern culture, we say we love all kinds of things that we really just strongly like. So, the word *phileo* implies a strong emotional connection or a deep friendship. It is definitely the feeling Jesus shared with his apostles. God has a strong emotional bond with us as well.

Then there is *eros*. It is the Greek word for romantic, sexual, or passionate love. It is not mentioned in the Bible, even though sexual passion is expressed very explicitly in the Song of Solomon. (That book was written in Hebrew, not Greek.) The true meaning of *eros* is slightly different than our modern term, *erotic*, because we often associate *erotic* with ideas or practices that are inappropriate. Instead, *eros is* described as the healthy, common expressions of physical love, primarily those expressions of love between a husband and wife.

The third word for love is *storge*. The Greeks used this word to mean "family love, the bond between mothers, fathers, sons, daughters, sisters, and brothers" (and grandkids, of course!). Just as with *eros*, *storge* is also not used by itself in the Bible. When *phileo* and *storge* are combined (*philostorgos*), it means loving dearly, being devoted, being very affectionate, loving in a way that is characteristic of the relationship in healthy families. I think many of us feel that same deep bond with our Christian brothers and sisters that we feel with our biological families. That's the beauty of the church!

The most complicated word translated as love is *agape*. *Agape* is not a feeling at all. It is love because of what it does, not because of how it feels. It is a willful action on behalf of another. "God so loved the world [*agape*] that he gave his only son" (John 3:16, ESV). God did not feel good about doing so, but to him, it was the loving thing to do. Likewise, Christ so loved us (*agape*) that he gave his life. He did not want to die, but because he loved us, he acted on what he needed to do.

Agape love is not simply an impulse in response to our feelings.

Instead, it is a willful, deliberate choice. It is loving another person when loving is the last thing you *feel* like doing. This is why God can command us to love our enemies (Matthew 5:44, ESV). He is not commanding us to have a *good feeling* for our enemies, but to act in a loving way toward them. *Agape* love is related to obedience and commitment, and not just feelings and emotions.

Loving someone the way God wants means that we are to seek that person's goodwill and blessing. You can tell someone you love them, but your words don't mean anything without your actions to confirm it. Think about it: lack of love invalidates your words. That is not just the ones you say, but those in print, in emails, texts, and on Facebook, Twitter, or other social media. That is why it is important to think about the motives of our hearts before we post anything.

One of the best-known Bible passages is 1 Corinthians 13. It is often called the "love chapter." It is read at many weddings every year, but its message about sacrificial *agape* love is important for all of us to remember. Starting with the fourth verse (ESV), it says, "Love is patient and kind; love does not envy or boast; it is not arrogant or rude. It does not insist on its own way; it is not irritable or resentful; it does not rejoice at wrongdoing but rejoices with the truth. Love bears all things, believes all things, hopes all things, endures all things."

Do those traits describe you? Do you love that way? I thought I did, but then a Christian sister challenged me to try a little experiment. She said that I should put my name in place of "love" throughout these verses. I felt embarrassed and sad as I read, "Diana is patient (well, some of the time), Diana is kind (I try to be), Diana does not envy, Diana does not boast, Diana is not arrogant or rude (it's getting harder). Diana does not insist on her own way (well …). Diana is not irritable or resentful (ouch!)." It was hard to continue! I want to be all those things, but I know I fall short. Try it for yourself. Be brave and honest with yourself. I sure have some things to pray about. How about you?

Someone posted this practical list online, and I just had to share with you. They are so good!

Ten ways to love:

- Listen without interrupting (Proverbs 18).
- Speak without accusing (James 1:19).
- Give without sparing (Proverbs 21:26).
- Pray without ceasing (Colossians 1:9).
- Answer without arguing (Proverbs 17:1).
- Share without pretending (Ephesians 4:15).
- Enjoy without complaining (Philippians 2:14).
- Trust without wavering (1 Corinthians 13:7).
- Forgive without punishing (Colossians 3:13).
- Promise without forgetting (Proverbs 13:12).

God wants us to model his love for the world in all we say and do. How else will they get to know him? We are to be his hands and feet to those who are hurting and hungry. Our actions will speak louder than our words. Remember, people don't care how much you know until they know how much you care. "A new commandment I give to you, that you love one another: just as I have loved you, you also are to love one another" (John 13:34, ESV). Why? Jesus tells us in Matthew 25:34–45 that when we do all those agape kind of things—feed the hungry, clothe the naked, welcome the stranger, visit those in prison, and so on, we are doing it to him. If we aren't, then we have no part in his kingdom.

Thankfully, we don't have to love by our own power. We have the power of the Holy Spirit living in us to fill us with love to overflowing. We are loved and then we love. That's all that it's about. Love. Period.

Grandma D.'s wisdom: I promise you that our Father loves you perfectly and completely. He knows when you struggle with loving others, and he loves you anyway. He adores everything about you. You are his masterpiece! His love never ever ends. Even if everyone else lets you down, he never will. You can lean on that promise. (And if you didn't read Psalm 139 yet, go do it now!)

Love (yes, love!), Grandma D.

Chapter 4

JOY, JOY, JOY, JOY DOWN IN MY HEART

When you read the title of this chapter, did you start singing that cute song you learned in your church youth group, vacation Bible school, or at summer camp? "I've got the joy, joy, joy, joy down in my heart! Where? Down in my heart! Where? Down in my heart. I've got the joy, joy, joy, joy down in my heart, down in my heart to stay!" I bet you are singing it right now, aren't you? (At least we used to sing that song in the "old" days!)

It would be nice if having joy in our lives was as easy as singing a song, wouldn't it? But the cares and worries of life seem to crowd out our joy. The reason for that is because we equate joy with happiness. That is the kind of joy the world wants—happy times, fun, laughter, and no problems to ever worry about. That is unrealistic as well as impossible. If we ever do experience that kind of joy, then it is only temporary. When our favorite teams lose another game, there goes our joy. When we misplace our car keys and are late for work, there goes our joy. When the person we voted for does not win the election, there goes our joy. When our children get in trouble at school, there goes our joy. When our spouses are unfaithful and want a divorce, there goes our joy. When we find out from the doctor that we have cancer, there goes our joy. Yes, many of our struggles and trials can cause us great concern, even to the point where we question how we can find joy in anything that is happening to us.

Circumstances can have a positive or negative impact on our joy *if* our joy is based on our feelings. True joy is the natural reaction to the work of God, whether it is promised in the future or already fulfilled. Joy expresses God's influence on earth, not our own works or actions. "For the kingdom of God is not a matter of eating and drinking (fun) but of righteousness and peace and joy in the Holy Spirit" (Romans 14:17, ESV).

It's interesting that the Greek word for joy is *chara*, which is closely related to *charis*, which means grace. My joy overflows because of God's grace. In fact, sometimes my joy is so great it cannot even be expressed. "Though you have not seen him, you love him; and even though you do not see him now, you believe in him and are filled with an inexpressible and glorious joy!" (1 Peter 1:8, NIV). That's the kind of joy I want all the time!

Having joy is a choice. We choose whether we want to value God's presence, his promises, and his continual working in our lives. When we yield to the Holy Spirit, he opens our eyes to God's grace around us and fills us with joy. "May the God of hope fill you with all joy and peace in believing, so that by the power of the Holy Spirit you may abound in hope" (Romans 15:13, ESV).

Robert Reid (not the actor) would have every reason to not have joy in his life. We would understand if he felt miserable and sorry for himself. His hands are twisted, and his feet are useless. His words form slowly, and he is difficult to understand because his speech is slurred. He cannot bathe or feed himself. Things we do easily, he cannot do—brush his teeth, comb his hair, or even put on his own underwear. Strips of Velcro hold his shirts together. Robert, you see, has cerebral palsy.

The disease keeps him from driving a car, riding a bike, and going for a walk. But it did not keep him from graduating high school or graduating from Abilene Christian University with a Bible degree in Latin. He even taught at a college and traveled overseas on five mission trips. In fact, in 1972, Robert did not let his disease prevent him from moving all alone to Lisbon, Portugal, to become a missionary. When he got there, he rented a hotel room and began studying Portuguese. He found a restaurant owner who would feed him every day after the rush hour and a tutor who would instruct him in the language. Then he planted himself daily in a park, where he handed out brochures about Christ. Within six years, he led seventy people to the Lord, one of whom became his wife, Rosa. He is known for holding his bent hand up in the air and boasting, "I have everything I need for joy! My shirts are held together by Velcro, but my life is held together by joy unspeakable! A joy so great words cannot describe it! There is leaping and dancing on the inside of me … one day in the future it will be on the outside of me, too!"

Can you imagine yourself in his place? How discouraging these circumstances could be. Think about it. What would be your response if this was the life you had to face every single day? Would your response be as positive as his? Would you be as joyful? I must admit that Robert's depth of faith and his response of joy are challenging for me. I have had many struggles, but nothing I have faced could come close to his experience. What is his secret?

Robert's joy comes from the Holy Spirit, not his circumstances. He is confident that his victory may not come until he meets the Lord, but it will come. God wants us to have a joy-filled life, too. The fruit of joyfulness is the Spirit's working power in our lives that helps us to have joy despite our circumstances. We look beyond the struggles, the grief, the battles, and the pain and know that ahead of us is victory. One day, just like Robert said, we will be dancing around the throne with no more suffering and sadness.

King Jehoshaphat, who was one of the faithful rulers of Judah, was a strong and wise man, one who served God with all his heart. He took away the idols that the people had been worshiping and turned the hearts of the people to the Lord. We read in 2 Chronicles 20 that one day the king received a message that an enemy army was coming against his people. He immediately did the right thing: he turned to the Lord and asked for help. He told all the people to pray and ask God to fight the battle for them. The people came from far away to the temple in Jerusalem, and the king stood and prayed to God. He knew that the armies coming against his people were greater than his own armies. In faith, he said to God, "We do not know what to do, but our eyes are upon you" (2 Chronicles 20:12, ESV). He told the people not to fear because the Lord would not let the enemy harm them. Then the spirit of the Lord caused one of the Levite priests to announce, "The battle is not yours, but God's. You will not need to fight in this battle: stand firm, hold your position, and see the salvation of the Lord on your behalf" (2 Chronicles 20:15, 17, ESV). The prophet told them to go out the next day and watch because the Lord would be with them.

Early the next morning, the people nervously started out to the battle. As they left, the king again encouraged them to believe in God. Then he appointed certain ones as singers to go out *in front* of the soldiers. This is the song they would sing: "Praise the Lord; for His mercy endures forever" (2 Chronicles 20:21, NKJV). The people of Judah did not have to do any fighting; the singers sang and praised the Lord. What happened? God caused the enemies to fight among themselves and all were destroyed! The battle was won, and all the people did was sing!

Did you know that the Greek word for worship, *Proskuneo*, means "kisses toward?" I just love that image! When I worship, it's as if I am blowing kisses to God, and he catches them and blows them right back to me in blessings!

That's why I love to sing and write music to praise God for his mercy and kindness toward me. When I sing, I give him praise, but I am also benefiting from the closeness I feel with him. The next time something makes you unhappy, lift your heart to Jesus and your voice in praise. Blow kisses by your worship and allow him to love you back. Even better, why not rejoice even before the battles come?

Paul tells us to rejoice in the Lord always. He believed it so much that he repeated the admonition: "I will say it again—Rejoice!" (Philippians 4:4. NIV). It does not mean only when everything is going my way, but also when things are upside down and overwhelming. And if Paul could model this joy during beatings, shipwrecks, and prison, I think he knew what he was talking about!

The apostle Peter tells us that our trials are more precious than *gold refined in fire*. First Peter 1:6–9 (NIV) says:

> In all this you greatly rejoice, though now for a little while you may have had to suffer grief in all kinds of trials. These have come so that the proven genuineness

of your faith—of greater worth than gold, which perishes even though refined by fire—may result in praise, glory, and honor when Jesus Christ is revealed. Though you have not seen him, you love him; and even though you do not see him now, you believe in him and are filled with inexpressible and glorious joy, for you are receiving the end result of your faith, the salvation of your souls.

You may not know about the ancient way that gold was refined and purified. First, gold was found and removed from the earth or from a riverbed. Then the refiner took over. He washed away all the sand and dirt and crushed the gold to break down the particles. He then put the gold bits into a clay pot, sealed it up, and placed it in the hottest fire possible for several days. When the pot was removed from the fire, the impurities and waste, called "dross," had risen to the top. The refiner then scraped them off and discarded them. If there were still more imperfections, he repeated this process until only the purest gold was left.

That is just like us, isn't it? God is searching for us. When he finds us, he washes us clean with the living water of Jesus. But then we are tested by struggles and challenges, and it feels like we are crushed. Sometimes we face difficult, fiery trials that heat us beyond what we think we can bear. But God knows that those tough times remove the impurities in us and lead us to become more like him, purified like gold. That is why we can rejoice in our sufferings because they bring us closer to him.

Jesus went through many difficult times throughout his life; he understood fiery trials even before he faced the cross. But the cross was more than just another trial. The cross was pain! It was intense suffering! It was the greatest agony known to mankind. How could Jesus endure the cross and the torment of that physical pain? I cannot grasp it. My heart breaks when I think about it.

In Hebrews 12:2 (NIV), we see that he endured the cross, even though he despised the pain, because of "the joy that was set before him." What was that joy that Jesus saw when he was on the cross? What was that deep joy that he focused upon when the pain was nearly too much to bear? He could have called ten thousand angels to take him out of that situation. Why didn't he stop it? The joy that gave Jesus the strength to stay hanging on that cross was you … and it was me.

Jesus knew that he had to die so that we could live. That was joy to him! Jesus knew that he had to be nailed on the cross so that we could be set free from pain, sorrow, and depression. He knew that his body had to bear the pain of a horrible death so that we could be healed. And he counted that as pure joy!

When I think about the cross of Calvary, I know that Jesus died a horrible, painful death to forgive me of my sins. I know beyond a shadow of a doubt that he died for every wrong choice I will ever make. As difficult as it is to fathom, I know that the cross was necessary for me to be forgiven and to live eternally with God. I can have joy because I have him. And so can you! It is sad that even though we know these things, we still sometimes forget. We forget how intensely he suffered. We forget that he was alone and that even his Father had turned away. We forget that he did this purely because he loved us.

Sometimes we just take Jesus's sacrifice for granted. Sometimes we forget the joy of our salvation and let other things crowd out remembering what he did for us. That precious gift should bring us great joy! We do not deserve it; we cannot earn it no matter how hard we try.

The joy of the Lord really is your strength. Satan knows that if he can rob you of your strength, he will turn you into a weak, whining, ineffective Christian. Satan is sly and sneaky. Even though it might feel like it, he is not after your health. Satan couldn't care less about your marriage or your finances or even your children. Those things mean nothing to him. What he is really after is your joy. The way he tries to steal your joy is by going after your health, your marriage, your finances, and your children.

The devil knows that he cannot take away your salvation or the forgiveness that Jesus has given to you. So what he tries to steal is the next most valuable thing you have—your joy. He is relentless and will do anything to lie to you and deceive you out of your joy. He will try to convince you that you are all alone, that no one can understand how bad your life is or how deep your pain is. He is a *liar*! Thankfully, Jesus understands; he has had quite a few run-ins with the devil over the centuries! Jesus has promised us that he will never leave us or forsake us. He says, "In this world you will have trouble. But take heart! I have overcome the world!" (John 16:33, NIV). So, one day we will be free from all pain and suffering. What joy we have before us! Of course, choosing to be a joyful Christian even when suffering extraordinary physical pain seems unrealistic in human eyes. How can anyone in his or her right mind consider trials to be a reason for joy? It is unthinkable … unless, of course, you know and put all your trust in Jesus.

My precious friend Arden is always in pain. It is not temporary. It is intense, constant, and long-lasting. It has been her life for many years. I cannot imagine how difficult it is for her—in and out of hospitals, unable even to eat food without pain, often too weak to enjoy simple activities. But Arden's faith is greater than her suffering. Her joy is in the Lord. Her strength is only in him. She does not define her life by her limits, but by the power of the Holy Spirit living in her. Her joyful response? She finds ways to bless those around her. She sends encouraging cards and notes to others nearly every day. In fact, I am sure there are hundreds of lives she has touched and changed by her words. Everyone who knows Arden smiles when you mention her name because she is a young woman who knows joy. She is an inspiration to me and to many others.

Arden would gladly tell you this truth: we can have joy regardless of trauma or tragedy because nothing is able to separate us from the presence of our heavenly Father. And it is in his presence where there is always fullness of joy. Neither death nor disease can deny us the strength and comfort of his presence. Financial ruin, relationship challenges, and even broken hearts do not have the power to remove his children from the Father's love and tender care. A divorce cannot deny you access to his love, and rebellious children will not keep you away from all that he is.

Arden knows better than many of us that this life is not about us! Joy is not just something that was invented to make us feel good. A life filled with godly joy will draw others to us because they will see something unique in us. Others will listen to us and want to know more because we have the joy that only salvation brings. We all want to make a difference in this world; we want our lives to count for more than just the dash between the dates on our tombstones. When we share joy with others, we are leaving a legacy. As their lives are changed, they can't help but share that joy with others, too. Despite our personal pains or struggles, true joy will enable us to make a difference in someone else's life.

One Bible commentator said it beautifully: "Joy is the deep-down sense of well-being that abides in the heart of the person who knows all is well between himself and the Lord. It is not an experience that comes from favorable circumstances or even a human emotion … It is God's gift to believers." And that is the reason why, when we live joy-filled lives, others are drawn to the Father.

With the Holy Spirit's help, we can choose joy in situations when joy would be our very last response. When we are angry with people or disappointed with life or in the throes of grief or even tormented by depression, James points us to a healthier alternative: *joy*! He says, "Consider it *pure joy* when you face trials of many kinds, because you know that the testing of your faith produces perseverance" (James 1:2–4, NIV). Perseverance helps us to become more like Jesus and live godly lives despite our struggles. God honors this as worship. Earthly circumstances can steal our happiness but never our joy!

All farmers and gardeners know that if you plant zucchini seeds, you will yield zucchini. You never get cucumbers or tomatoes or corn or pineapples or anything else. But in God's garden, there is one exception: when you sow in tears, you will always reap with shouts of joy (Psalm 126:5–6 ESV).

If you have cried yourself to sleep too many times to count, or if you have experienced the sorrow of depression, disappointment, and sadness, do not give up! Your tears have fertilized the seeds of joy that God has planted in the garden of your life. Those who have sown the tears of tragedy and pain have the greatest capacity for joy! It may not always feel like it, but God has not forgotten you. One of my favorite verses is Psalm 56:8 (NLT), which says, "You keep track of all my sorrows. You have collected all my tears in your bottle. You have recorded each one in your book." He knows every tear we have ever cried and each one that we will cry in the future. I know my bottle of tears is already a full one! What comfort there is in knowing how much he cares! He wants to turn our sadness into a bountiful harvest of joy!

I start every day rejoicing that his mercies never come to an end. They are new every morning. I can do that only by reminding myself that God is in control of all the details of my life. Joy is the confidence that ultimately everything is going to be all right. It is the determined choice to praise God in every situation. Joy—it's down in my heart to stay!

Grandma D.'s wisdom: A heart filled with joy is one that fully trusts that God is in control. It even makes you more beautiful on the outside, too. You are more peaceful, more confident, and there is a spring in your step. And that beautiful smile of yours? It's dazzling! So, choose joy, my dear child.

Love, Grandma D.

Chapter 5

A PIECE OF PEACE

It seems like every time I watch the Miss America Pageant, one of those smiling contestants always gushes, "I just want world peace." But peace is much more than a platitude. It is more than the absence of conflict. It is even more than what the world says: "an internal response to outward circumstances." You see, everyone wants to find peace. Whether it is with meditation or medication, peace still seems to be elusive. The goal is to find true "inner peace"—a state of internal calm and self-acceptance.

The self-help gurus tell us that if you have peace, you can transcend past regrets and future worries. You are not bothered by the behavior of others. The struggles and worries of life will simply fade into the background. That is easier said than done, isn't it? The problem is that inner peace comes from, well, within. It requires us to focus daily on achieving peace, to master our self-wills, to train our minds, and to eliminate negativity. But no matter how strong my will may be, I cannot always control it. Inner peace has limits if I am doing it on my own.

When my children, Leslie and Ryan, were in elementary school, I decided they needed alarm clocks in their rooms to help them get ready for school. My goal was to teach them responsibility. It seemed only right that they should wake themselves up in the mornings. Leslie was not thrilled about this. She knew that when Mom called the first three or four times, she had at least another ten minutes before she really had to get up.

Ryan was excited because he wanted to pick out his own alarm clock. I should have known that this excitement would not last long! The first morning was a mother's dream come true. Both children woke up cheerfully and jumped out of bed with smiles on their faces. They were excited at the prospect of another day of school and hurriedly put their clothes on. They ate breakfast and brushed their teeth without prompting. Off we drove to school, early, and with smiles on our faces.

Of course, this dream did not last long. A few days later, the scenario went more like this: Leslie woke up yelling at Ryan because his alarm was too loud and had been blasting for ten minutes. Ryan stumbled out of bed, turned off his alarm, and promptly went back to sleep. About fifteen minutes before it was time to go, I cheerfully walked into Ryan's room expecting his fully clothed, bed-made-breakfast-eaten-everything's-right-with-the-world greeting and instead found him snoring away. I let out a shriek of panic, jerked back the covers, and yanked him to the floor. I threw clothes at him, all the time reminding him of the purpose of an alarm clock and his responsibility. I was so angry and frustrated that I began to cry. My peace didn't just jump out the window, it went running down the block!

I think back to that chaotic morning and realize that the turmoil I felt was not Ryan's fault, but my response to the situation. It is easy to feel peaceful when things are going okay. But how can I feel peace on those hectic, we're-gonna-be-late days? I would like just a little piece of peace, but somehow, I have a large slice of tension. If you still have children at home, I am sure you can relate. Peace often seems elusive, doesn't it?

Our lives are like this in so many ways. It may not be an alarm clock, but other problems blare at us just as loudly! It may be a phone call from the school principal or a late notice in the mail or a discouraging call from the doctor. It can be something even more serious—conflicts with our spouses or even the death of a loved one. How can we have true godly, Spirit-filled peace no matter what hits us from day to day?

Sometimes we think we cannot find peace because we just have too much to worry about. We women are such worriers, aren't we? We worry about big things, like the state of the world, or small things, like what we should fix for dinner. There are the daily worries that can sap our energy: we worry about our children when they are at school. We worry about our husbands when they are at work. We worry about our parents, our friends, and our jobs. Our sensitive, loving hearts just want to hurt for others, don't they? If you are single, you may worry about getting married someday. Will that right person ever come along? If you have struggled with infertility, you worry that you may never be a parent. Sometimes our worries, even our serious ones, can just spiral out of control. Jesus tells us to stop it! Stop worrying! "Can anyone of you by worrying add a single hour to your life?" (Matthew 6:27, NIV). Sometimes "just stop worrying" seems easier said than done.

I know there are some real concerns we may have to face—cancer, divorce, grief, addiction, and yes, infertility. Thankfully, God understands our human hearts. We do not have to deny that our worries exist. But at the same time, we must realize that we have a Father who is deeply in love with us. He wants to take those worries from us and give us his peace.

If we believe that God is good and that he cares about us, then we have to believe Jesus when he tells us to not worry or be afraid. "Peace I leave with you; my peace I give you. I do not give to you as the world gives. Do not let your hearts be troubled and do not be afraid" (John 14:27, NIV). His peace is not the kind we try to manage on our own human strengths. His peace can be ours even when those serious problems tear at our hearts.

My dear friend Katie and her husband, Vince, lost their sweet two-year-old baby boy, Charlie, a few months ago to a rare and painful disease known as HLH. Charlie was a bubbly, happy baby who was very sick for most of his time on this earth. Of course, Katie, Vince, and thousands of people around the world prayed for God to heal this precious little guy. We were all heartbroken when God didn't answer our prayers the way we had hoped. It was hard to understand. Even now, grieving Charlie is very real and raw, but Katie has a beautiful perspective that comes only from a life in tune with a loving Father. I can't say it any better than Katie can. Here are her words:

> Do you know what's most beautiful about the reminders of Charlie? It's that each reminder of him is coupled with a reminder of the Lord's faithfulness. There's

simultaneous grief because of loss and worship because of the love and tenderness of the Lord. Moving forward into more uncertain times, I'm so grateful. What the Lord cemented in my heart was not that "everything's going to be okay" or "we can get through this," because those are dependent upon circumstances, or even worse, our own strength. What he cemented was that he is the prize. If Charlie had not lived and died, would I have known that Jesus is the true prize? I don't know, honestly, but I can tell you now that even after losing my son, Jesus is the prize. I'm not different because of the grief, I'm different because of how Jesus entered into the grief and overwhelmed me with peace. This is available to all different kinds of grief and pain. It's not theoretical or abstract."

Katie learned a powerful lesson amid a mother's greatest pain. And she knows that same hope and peace are available to you, no matter what you are going through. Jesus can be your prize, too.

Think about it—we have a Savior who experienced anguish himself. There was that long night in the garden of Gethsemane when his heart was heavy with despair. He was in so much torment that it knocked him to his knees, and he prayed intensely for hours over what was ahead of him. He knew he was about to take on all the sins of the entire world in the most horrendous, painful death. He prayed for a way out. He wanted his Father to just take the suffering away from him, to provide another way. But God didn't do that. There was not another way out because Jesus was the way—the only way who could give us hope, salvation, and a real relationship with God as our Father. So, Jesus submitted, "Not my will, but yours, be done" (Luke 22:42, ESV). Then God gave him the strength and peace he needed to take our sins upon himself.

How can we, like Jesus, turn our worries into worship? How can we find that deep peace? Is there some godly advice to help us with our worries? The answer is not for me to just say to you, "Now, don't you worry," and pat you on the head. We need a road map, a divine "peace plan" that is built on confidence and a relationship with the one who knows our needs better than we do. This plan can help us when worry and dread creep into our thoughts. It can give us hope amid our fears and doubts.

Ideally, it is helpful to have this plan in place *before* those worries and stresses confront us. My whole day changes when I implement my peace plan first thing every morning. That plan is just my way of reminding myself of the power the Holy Spirit gives me to cope with any and every situation. So, my first step every morning is to spend time with the true peacemaker—my heavenly Father. I ask him for wisdom to handle all the stressful situations that may arise that day.

Sometimes we need to feel his peace during a long struggle that never seems to end, and other times, something might just sneak up on us and knock us breathless to the ground. The answer, like Katie said, is to ask him to just let us feel his presence. He promises never to leave us without his peace and comfort.

I also pray about my attitude. Will I let circumstances control me or the Spirit? Spending time every day in God's word also gives me extra strength and peace. I am always amazed at how he continually speaks to my deepest need at just the perfect time. To accomplish this, it means I must get up earlier, so I do not have to rush through my time with him. But it is time well-spent. After all, I cannot experience the Spirit's fruit if I am not staying connected to the vine!

So, when worry and stress start to creep in anyway, what do we do? Paul gives us some practical wisdom: "Do not be anxious about anything, but in every situation, by prayer and petition, with thanksgiving, present your requests to God. And the peace of God, which transcends all understanding, will guard your hearts and your minds in Christ Jesus" (Philippians. 4:6–7 NIV).

That is smart advice. When you start to fret, stop immediately, take a deep breath, and pray. Let your requests and praises just calm you down. Yes, those thankful praises really do help! Even if your worry is justifiable and serious, stop the thought as soon as it comes to your mind. If you do not stop, it can lead to stress, exhaustion, and weakness. Then pray, pray, pray!

Now, there is not a prescription for how you have to pray. You do not need fancy words. Just talk to him like you talk to your best friend. Tell

God your concerns and just offer them up to him. Release them into his care and your heart into his loving arms. If the worry is too consuming, just lie down on your bed and let him hear your heart and your tears. Remember how much he loves you. By the way, he can handle anything you say to him—even your greatest fears and anger. (He already knows them anyway!)

It is not by our own strength that we can stop worrying; it is the Holy Spirit who gives us his supernatural peace. He is the one who helps us to stop the cycle. When we do that, his peace can replace our worries. We just need to stand up to them and stop them as soon as they hit. That way, we can thank God even on our darkest days. Some days you may not feel like thanking and praising God, but do it even if you don't feel it. That is the substance of faith. With that release you will find a sense of his peace that will soon start to coat your life and your heart like honey.

What else can help me hang on to peace when life is out of control and "unpeaceful?" We all have stories of how the events of 2020 changed our lives. Whether it was the pandemic, the political climate, the social unrest and violence, the hurricanes, wildfires, or even—so scary!—homeschooling our children, it was not a year anyone would call peaceful!

Yes, there have been many events in our world, not only those in 2020, that have caused us stress. As I get older, I see more and more evil around me. Sadly, so many people are focusing on their own needs and wants. Hatred, anger, violence, and greed are consuming them, and our society is suffering because of it. It is hard to feel peace when everything is unpredictable, isn't it? But to live peacefully, we must regularly remind ourselves that Satan is not in control even when it feels like he is. He is the father of lies, and he is trying to defeat us in many ways. The Holy Spirit has given us the gift of his peacefulness. He does not give it and then take it away! Praying and staying in the Word of God can help us keep our focus where it should be.

If I focus on any stress that arises, I can easily feel overwhelmed. Instead, I need to focus on how deeply I am loved and how much he has already done for me. Finding *the right perspective* is essential. When I start to feel worried or stressed, I remind myself of all those other tough times that I was guided and strengthened by a heavenly source. I have experienced many such incidents—when my first husband had two difficult brain surgeries for epilepsy, when my mother was diagnosed with cancer, or when my dear father died unexpectedly at only fifty-nine.

Dealing with those personal stresses gave me strength and peace to handle even greater struggles—when Bill later died from his seizures, or when my sister (my only sibling) and my sweet mama died six months apart. Or, even more recently, when I contracted COVID-19 and was on a breathing machine in ICU for two weeks. As difficult as all these were, I was ministered to and comforted by God. He led me through each storm to a place of peace and rest. As I was going through these trials, they were often staggering, but when I reminded myself or others reminded me of God's presence, then I was able to hold on and have peace.

A godly perspective helps us to remember that he has never failed us before, and he will certainly not fail us now! He knows the future. He is already there. I love this little poem. I remember my mama reciting it many times over the years. I think she used it to remind herself not to worry and to rely on God's presence.

O You of Little Faith

O you of little faith,
God has not failed you yet!
When all looks dark and gloomy,
How soon you do forget—
Forget that He has led you,
And gently cleared your way;
On clouds has poured His sunshine,
And turned your night to day.
And if He's helped you thus before,
He will not fail you now.
How it must wound His loving heart
To see your anxious brow!
Oh, doubt not any longer,
To Him commit your way,

Whom in the past you trusted
Is "just the same" today!
(Author Unknown)

Every day I thank God for his blessings, reminding myself of all the ways he has worked in my life and not ever, ever forsaken me. You see, it took me many years to figure it out—the peace of Christ is not found by looking for it, but by looking at it. His peace is found when I keep my eyes on him. Just like the words of one of my favorite hymns, "Turn your eyes upon Jesus. Look full in his wonderful face. And the things of earth will grow strangely dim in the light of his glory and grace" (Helen Howarth Lemmel, 1922).

The prophet Isaiah said, "You keep him in perfect peace whose mind is stayed on you, because he trusts in you. Trust in the Lord forever, for the Lord God is an everlasting rock!" (Isaiah 26:3–4, ESV). Yes, he is the only rock you can stand on when the waves of doubt and worry want to knock you down. Even if it seems overwhelming, keep reminding yourself that he can be trusted. He is unwavering. He loves you. Keep your mind staying, resting on him.

In both Mark 4 and Matthew 8, there is the story of a wild storm that came up suddenly on the Sea of Galilee. Jesus's disciples were trying to navigate their boat to the other shore, but the winds were rocking the boat almost to the point of it sinking. These men, including some professional fishermen who had been on that sea many times, were all terrified. But Jesus? He was sleeping peacefully.

Whenever I read that story, I always wonder: Why didn't they wake Jesus sooner? Maybe they thought that everything would be okay. Did they think their boat was big enough? Or maybe the storm was small enough? Or possibly their abilities were good enough to manage the storm on their own? Whatever their reason, they let Jesus sleep. We are like that, too. Why don't we ask Jesus to calm our storms? Could it be that we think we can handle them on our own, that we don't need his help? We believe we are strong enough, capable enough, and smart enough. But are we really? Nothing we have and nothing we can do will ever give us the peace only God can provide.

Maybe we have just given up on having peace. We have been in storm after storm, and it is just the way our lives are meant to be—always filled with stress and chaos. We think we can never have peace in our lives because there really is no such thing. But Jesus, our prince of peace, waits to calm our storms and give us his peace in our lives. We just need to ask.

Or could it be that we have given up on God? After all, we think, Jesus has been asleep in this boat before. It seems like we have prayed and prayed without any answers. We have felt all alone, grieving hopelessly, suffering helplessly, so we just keep rowing on our own. At least, it has always felt that way, so we let him sleep. But all that time, he has been waiting for us to turn to him.

So where are you? Are you rowing with all your strength against the storms? Is the wind whipping in your face and taking your breath away? Peace comes when you let Jesus be the captain of your boat. He wants to take the helm at the beginning of every storm and give you his peace. He can carry you through anything because he has overcome it all; true peace is in Jesus alone. "I have told you these things, so that in me you may have peace. In this world you will have trouble. But take heart! I have overcome the world" (John 16:33, NIV). One of my favorite Christian songs reminds me:

Sometimes He Calms the Storm

Sometimes He calms the storm
With a whispered peace be still.
He can settle any sea,
But it doesn't mean He will
Sometimes He holds us close,
And lets the wind and waves go wild.
Sometimes He calms the storm,
And other times He calms His child.
(Scott Krippayne, 1995)

Besides struggling with life's worries and trials, it can be hard for us to find peace when we feel the weight of our sins. Sometimes it feels like Satan is goading us, reminding us that we are guilty, that we don't deserve forgiveness, and that we just aren't good enough! We want to tell him to stop it, but we know our sins and they feel heavy on our hearts. Wouldn't it be wonderful if our mistakes could be erased forever? What if we could actually have peace without fear or guilt taunting us? Wouldn't that be awesome?

Oh, but there is such peace! It was given to us by Jesus on the cross. It is God's promise of forgiveness, refined by the Holy Spirit in our lives. It takes away all that fear and guilt and gives us his peace. It is God's incomparable free gift! If you are a Christian, then you can rest assured that he has forgiven you and made you white as snow. Do not let past guilt take away your peace! You are his precious child now and forever.

If you haven't made Jesus the Lord of your life, then you have been doing it on your own for too long! You don't have access to that perfect peace that is found only in a relationship with him. How can you get that relationship? It's not really complicated, but it is life changing. First, you confess your belief that Jesus truly is the Son of God. Then you are baptized (immersed in water), and your sins are washed away. As you come up out of the water, you are made new and clean. All that guilt, all those mistakes, all that fear—gone! Not only that, but you receive the gift of the Holy Spirit living inside you! That is some gift! The apostle Peter made it simple: "Repent and be baptized, every one of you, in the name of Jesus Christ for the forgiveness of your sins. And you will receive the gift of the Holy Spirit" (Acts 2:38, ESV).

As a new Christian, you become a daughter of the King! You can know without a doubt that you are his beloved child, and he has prepared for you a home in heaven. That love, that acceptance, can give you true peace. "The peace of God, which surpasses all understanding, will guard your hearts and your minds in Christ Jesus" (Philippians 4:7, ESV). Yes, his peace truly is beyond our understanding. He died for us to have it!

Whether we are consumed with guilt or worry, or if life sometimes knocks us off our feet, we need to remind ourselves that we always have a loving Savior who wants to take those worries and fill us with his perfect peace. It is not just a little "piece" of peace; his arms are full of love and grace. He held his arms wide open on the cross. It was his way of telling us that he truly loves us. Yes, he loves you that much!

Grandma D.'s wisdom: My dear child, I know that life can be pretty overwhelming. Are you struggling with worry, doubt, and fear? Is your boat about to tip over? Jesus really wants to calm your storms and give you his peace from the inside out. You just have to let him! I promise you, there is nothing better. I'm praying for you!

Love, Grandma D.

Chapter 6

ANNOYING AN OYSTER

You may be familiar with the story about how oysters make pearls. We have heard that a grain of sand gets inside the shell and is not dispelled. Actually, it is not usually a grain of sand, but another type of irritant, such as an organism or even a piece of food. Whatever it is, the oyster does not like this uninvited visitor because of the discomfort it causes. It secretes a substance called nacre, also known as mother-of-pearl. To protect itself from the irritation, the oyster will quickly begin covering the pest with layers and layers of nacre. After some time, this painful process will form a beautiful pearl.

I love pearls. A few years ago, while spending time on a mission trip in Beijing, China, I was fortunate to visit their pearl market. It was a huge building. My local friend, who knew all about the market, escorted us past all the merchants up to the top floor where there was a small, private shop displaying the most beautiful saltwater pearls of many different colors, shapes, and sizes. The owner showed us how to pick the best, most perfectly shaped ones. We picked out our own pearls, and then some very skilled young ladies hand-strung them for us. What a memorable experience. I brought home some breathtaking pearls that are still a treasure to me. One set I wore on my wedding day, and then my daughter wore them at her wedding. They will now be passed down to my granddaughters to wear at their weddings someday, and hopefully they will be worn for generations to come even after I am gone.

But the story of how a pearl is formed is one that amazes me. When that irritant gets inside the oyster, usually it can expel it. Sometimes it tries to get rid of it, but it can't. It is irritated and uncomfortable and just cannot do it. It locates the source of its pain, and the process begins. That pearl is the fruit of a frustrated oyster!

We are God's masterpieces; we are his pearls of great price. But there is a process. We cannot become a pearl without the struggles, pain, and conflict that arise in our lives. These struggles put us in the waiting room of patience. How you navigate your season of sowing determines your season of blessing.

Even though patience is a fruit of the Holy Spirit, it is one that most of us do not really want to talk about. But it is the one that most of us admit we struggle with. In fact, everyone I talked to personally said patience was something he or she has a problem with! My daughter said she has stopped praying for patience because when she did pray for it, God gave her twins! (But they are such sweet darlings anyway).

In some translations of the Bible, the list of the fruit of the Spirit in Galatians 5:22–23 uses the word *forbearance* for patience, which has a bit deeper meaning. *Forbearance* also includes self-control, restraint, and tolerance, implying that we have a choice about how we respond to God and others in our times of waiting.

In Greek, the word for patience as mentioned in this Galatians passage is *makrothumia*. It is a compound formed by *makros* (where we get the word *macro*, meaning big or long) and *thumos* (which means passion or temper and is also the root of the word for thermometer). Patience in Galatians 5:22 literally means "long temper" or "the ability to hold one's temper for a long time." The King James Version translates it as "longsuffering." A patient person can endure much pain and suffering without complaining. Someone once described patience this way: "It is a calm *endurance* based on the certain knowledge that God is in control." Since it is a fruit of the Spirit, we can possess *makrothumia* only through the power and work of the Holy Spirit in our lives.

Developing patience is challenging for us because it goes against human nature. We were not born patient, were we? When a baby wakes up in the middle of the night, it's almost always for one of two reasons— the child is either hungry or has a wet diaper. He or she does not just lie there and think, *I know Mommy and Daddy are tired, so I'll just wait until a more convenient time to let them know that I need something.* No, the baby squalls impatiently until someone comes in to meet his or her need! The child wants help and wants it right now!

It is not just babies; our children are not very patient, either. Have you ever traveled with a young child? That can be quite an experience, even more so if you have multiple children in the car! Little four-year-old Kevin was traveling with his mother, and he constantly asked her the same question repeatedly. "When are we going to get there? When are we going to get there?" Finally, his mother got so irritated that she said, "We still have ninety more miles to go. Do not ask me again when we're going to get there." Well, Kevin was silent for a long time. Then he timidly asked, "Mom, will I still be four when we get there?" He really wanted to be patient, but he was a bit worried.

We all face situations that try our patience daily: the kids are climbing the walls, you are stuck on hold with customer service, or the Wi-Fi is painfully slow. Living in America, the country that invented fast food, makes waiting for anything a challenge. Fast food was not fast enough, so we invented the drive-thru to get it faster. Now we even have the double drive-thru because we "need" it now! Max Lucado has said, "We are the only country with a mountain named Rushmore!" Researchers say if it takes more than 2.5 seconds for a web page to load, we close it and go to a different page. If the person walking in front of us does not move fast enough, we won't wait longer than 1.5 seconds before we pass them by! Pretty sad, isn't it? We do not want patience; we want action.

Speaking of children, the Israelites acted like little children when they fled from Egypt. When the soldiers and chariots were chasing them and they arrived at the Red Sea, what did the Israelites do? In Exodus 14:11 (NIV), they complained and cried, "Was it because there were no graves in Egypt that you brought us to the desert to die? What have you done to us?" Then Moses replied in verse thirteen, "Do not be afraid. Stand firm and you will see the deliverance the Lord will bring you today. The Egyptians you see today you will never see again."

The best part comes in verse fourteen. It is such an important verse. Moses said, "The Lord will fight for you; you need only to *be still*." I bet you're shaking your head, thinking, "C'mon Grandma D., I'm a mom. There is no such thing as being still!" But godly stillness means I'm going to wait for him to act. It is critical that we be still and wait on the Lord when it comes to the big stuff in our lives, because our God can handle it. Remember this formula: God's way + God's timing = God's blessing.

I was driving to a doctor appointment the other day after I had been studying and praying about this chapter on patience. You know what happens when you pray about patience, right? God puts obstacles in your path to help grow your patience. I hit every light red. The slower drivers were always right in front of me no matter which lane I was in. Just so you know, not all of us grandmothers drive like snails. I really have to keep an eye on my speedometer! When I got to the doctor's office, I was barely on time, and then I still had to wait for the doctor to see me! On the way home, I was a bit frustrated and said, "Lord, why is patience so hard? There isn't even a hymn to sing about patience!" But, of course, our wise, all-knowing God immediately popped a song in my head:

Teach Me Lord to Wait

Teach me Lord to wait
Down upon my knees,
Until your own good time
You will answer my pleas.
Teach me not to rely
On what others do,
But to wait in prayer
For an answer from you.
(Stuart Hamblen, 1953)

Then that beautiful song quotes Isaiah 40:31 (NIV): "They who wait upon the LORD shall renew their strength; they shall mount up with wings like eagles; they shall run and not be weary; they shall walk and not faint." Teach me, Lord, to wait!

Think about it: an eagle has such a wide wingspan that it has the ability to fly higher than most birds. It can fly longer distances. Because it flies so high, it can also see farther. You, dear one, were equipped to fly higher! You were built to go longer distances. You are gifted by God to mount up above life's problems and soar above the turbulence of this world. God has given you talents, abilities, and gifts that need to be developed, sharpened, and matured by him. It is in the waiting that we get our strength! Let me say that again: It is in the waiting that we get our strength! Trust God at every level. The more you exalt him in your life, the more your perspective changes. As you yield to his leading and his plan, the circumstances of life will not knock you off course.

James, the brother of Jesus, has much to say about patience. In James 5:7–11, he talks about the different kinds of patience we need. We need *patience with circumstances* (verse seven), just like the farmer waiting for his crops. In the old days, there were no irrigation systems, so the farmer had to wait for the rain and watch the weather to know the best time to plant. He could not rush it. The timing had to be just right; the only way he could have a bountiful harvest was by waiting for the rain.

What else might we need to wait for? Depending on where we are in our lives, there are many things. Are you waiting to find the right person to marry? Stand firm. Do not lower your standards and settle for the wrong person. Are you waiting for the right job or waiting for your finances to improve? When we try to force things our way and by our timing, we usually regret it. When we wait for God's way and his timing, the result will be God's blessings. He is always working and keeping his promises. And there is blessing and growth in the waiting!

Next, we need to have *patience with people* (verse nine). This is probably one of the most challenging problems for us. We can be quick to anger and grumble. It is not just about the lines at Target or that slow traffic in front of us (that's my frustration!). It is crucial for us to have patience with all people. We need patience with our spouses, our children, our parents, our siblings, our coworkers,, with strangers, and even with our Christian brothers and sisters with whom we might not always agree. James says God is the judge who will make everything right. Since God has been patient with me, I need to be the same with others. He has been patient with me one hundred, two hundred, a thousand times, and more (actually, a whole lot more)!

Going back to my lack of patience when driving, I find that I am more impatient and more verbal about it when I am in the car by myself. Can you relate? As I think about that, however, I realize that I am never really by myself. Why do I think it is acceptable to be impatient when my family is not in the car with me? If I want to improve my spiritual walk, then I need to work on my patience and responses all the time. Even if the responses are in my head and not coming out of my mouth, they are not helping me to become more godly, are they?

Then we also need *patience with God*. God's timing is different from ours. Think about how long Abraham waited after God told him he would be the father of all nations. He had to wait until he was ninety-eight to have a child with Sarah. Moses was forty when he went into exile, and he did not go back to Egypt until he was eighty. I am sure he was wondering about what God's purpose for his life could be, hanging out in Midian all those years. Then, one day there was a burning bush, and he found out. And what a purpose God had for him!

I know I told you before about my first husband, Bill, and his severe epilepsy. From the time he was a little boy, it had a huge impact on his life. It was even more challenging for our marriage and family. I prayed every day for more than twenty-five years that God would take those seizures away. In all those years of praying, I wondered why God, in my eyes, was not answering me. It felt like he was just ignoring me. I know now that he had answered my prayers repeatedly, but I just wasn't listening. I wasn't ready or willing to accept his answer.

Patience with God means we are going to trust that he loves us and knows what is best. Those many years of praying and waiting helped me to become more understanding of others who struggle with health issues, marital conflicts, family violence, and yes, even grief. You see, one day, God did answer my prayers. He took away those seizures forever when Bill went to his home in heaven.

That brings me to another kind of patience we need—*patience with suffering*. In verse eleven, James tells us to remain steadfast in our suffering, whether it is in pain from illness or from loss. God's ultimate purpose for our lives is not to get us out of pain, but to make us become more like him. The empty places in our hearts were created to be filled by God alone. The deepest thirst of our souls can be quenched only by him. The Lord is full of compassion and mercy. He is right there with us in our suffering. Like I mentioned above, I learned so much in the many years living with Bill's seizures. I could not understand what good could come from that painful struggle until a few years later when I had a little boy in my kindergarten class who had seizures. Because of my experience and my calm response, that little boy was always safe, and all the other children were never afraid or uneasy around him. That is just one example of many. God frequently used my pain to minister to others.

We all are impatient; we want to solve problems quickly. The way God perfects patience in us is to put us in places to wait—like with our spouses or children. Our patience runs thin when our children keep asking a dozen more times after we said *no* the first two times. Because we are that way, we mistakenly think God is just like us and loses his patience with us. But thankfully, he never wears out! No matter how far off the mark you feel you may be, God will hang with you as you grow and change. You see, God promises us that he will be patient with us as long as it takes! In 2 Peter 3:9 (NIV), it says, "The Lord is not slow in keeping his promise, as some understand slowness. He is patient with you, not wanting anyone to perish, but everyone to come to repentance."

When Paul writes to young Timothy, he wants to encourage him to remain strong and hold firm in his faith. Paul knows that God's patience is not just "good" patience, it is 100 percent perfect. There is not one bit of his patience that is not complete. Paul still remembered the weight of his own sins. In fact, he called himself the worst of all sinners. Then he told Timothy, "But for that very reason I was shown mercy so that in me, the worst of sinners, Christ Jesus might display his immense patience as an example for those who would believe in him and receive eternal life" (1 Timothy 1:16 NIV). In other words, if God had enough patience to forgive Paul, save him, and use him, then he has you covered!

Paul is not the only demonstration of God's patience. There are many other stories throughout the Bible. Of course, we all have heard about the patience of Job. He was steadfast even when everything was dark. In just one day, he lost all his businesses, had a funeral with ten caskets after all his children died, and his body was covered with painful boils. His wife told him to curse God and die. But he said, "Can we accept only good things from the hand of God and never anything bad?" (Job 2:10, NLT). Later, after being nagged and condemned repeatedly by his three "friends," he proclaimed, "I know my Redeemer lives, and he will stand upon the earth at last" (Job 19:25, NLT). He knew that even when God is silent, he is still faithful. He let what he *knew* outweigh what he *felt*!

When I look in the rearview mirror of my life, I see how God has loved and protected me so many times. It is a reminder that each day is a gift. I may feel discouraged today, but I know he lives! I may feel lonely or sad, but I know he lives! I may feel emotional or physical pain, but I know he lives! Remember, God is up to something in your life, too. Be patient! Take your worry, pain, and impatience to his throne. He knows, he understands, and he loves you, impatient or not!

As hard as we try, patience does not come from mental exercises, deep breathing, or trying harder. It comes as Jesus grows in our lives and as we trust and surrender every day.. Remind yourself about this: "I have lived only _____ years, but God has lived for eternity." You cannot see the future, but God can. How small and limited our perspectives are compared to his! He is loving, faithful, and good, and he is in control. After surviving a Nazi prison camp, Corrie ten Boom, said, "Never be afraid to trust an unknown future to a known God."

Did you know that from the beginning of time, there has been a war for your soul? In the garden of Eden, at the ark, in the wilderness, and in years of captivity, Satan thought he won. By the close of the Old Testament, there were four hundred years of silence—four hundred years of waiting! Then the New Testament opened. God made a move to destroy Satan's hold for all time. He came to Earth himself and became a baby. Satan was probably laughing at that, but he did not laugh for long. God's plan was perfect. Jesus took our places and gave us salvation, even though we did not deserve or earn it. If God has worked for that long to bring about his plan of redemption, he will be patient with your life to help you change into what he wants you to be, which really is the best anyway.

So, what does he want from you? He wants you to yield to his will. As you are rising to soar on wings like an eagle, remember that God himself is the wind that lifts you up. Place him at the forefront of your mind, thoughts, and actions. He is preparing to use you for something beyond what you can imagine. But he also promises to give you the strength and ability to do so. Have patience. Trust God. Do not faint. You were created for this. Soar high!

> *Grandma D's wisdom: Struggling with patience really is a part of our lives. I have learned, after many years of practice, that I have to stop the cycle of frustration immediately. I tell myself that all my uptight feelings, my worries, and my impatience will not really change anything. Can I make the car in front of me move faster? Nope. Can I get the doctor to see me sooner? Nope. Can I have the answers I want from God right now? Not likely. God works on his timeframe, not mine. It's the same with anything else we are waiting on. So, my dear, take a deep breath, say a prayer, and trust that God will work all things for your good.*
>
> *Love, Grandma D.*

Chapter 7

A NET OF KINDNESS

Sometimes it seems like everyone is in a hurry—rushing here and there and not really paying attention to what is happening around them. Sadly, this means we just don't "see" people who are struggling, who are lonely, or who are hungry for someone to show them a little kindness. They feel invisible. Have you ever felt that way?

That is why the "random acts of kindness" movement started, to encourage people to be kind to strangers. It is a feel-good action that we do to help someone else, and, in turn, it gives us the warm fuzzies. This might include helping an elderly woman cross a busy street or giving food to the homeless guy on the corner or paying for the person behind you in the drive-thru line at McDonald's (or in Texas, it has to be Whataburger!). If you google it, you will find many "feel good" quotes and ideas on how to be "random." In fact, there is an official "random acts of kindness week!" The purpose is twofold—you bestow a kind act on someone, then you will feel better about yourself.

I never dreamed that just last night, my own example of kindness would be found in a net! I promise you this story is 100 percent true! We live in the country—well, sort of. It is an unincorporated area that still has lots of homes. But because we are not in the city, we have all sorts of critters around us.

Last night, I took my little dogs out at about nine o'clock for their last potty break before bedtime. We have a swimming pool. A couple of weeks ago, our little miniature schnauzer puppy, Brody, leaned forward a bit too far and fell into the pool. We quickly discovered that not all dogs can swim! Ever since that scary incident, we have watched him cautiously to prevent him from taking another dive. He flies out of the house so quickly and hits the brakes right at the edge of the pool. So, when we go out at night, I turn on all the outdoor lights, including the one in the pool. Many nights, there are frogs swimming around. Last night, as I noticed the rippling of the water, I just knew it was another frog. But as I looked closer, to my surprise, I discovered it was just a cricket.

Now, I want you to understand, I dislike crickets immensely. They give me the creeps. I think my disgust of them started in college. When I was a student living in the dorm at Abilene Christian University, we always had hundreds of crickets crawling around on the ground under the lights by the doors. To get into the building, you had to expertly maneuver so as not to step on any. There is nothing more sickening than that *crunch* when you step on one!

So, finding a cricket squirming frantically in my pool was disheartening. I could easily have let him drown and get sucked up in the filter. One less cricket would not be the end of the world. I do not know why, but I thought about kindness. He was way over in the middle at the back side of the pool where I could not reach him. I got out the net, but not the pole to attach it to. Mind you, I was not going to work that hard. I stood there and said, "Okay, Lord, if I'm supposed to be kind and rescue this yucky cricket, make sure he gets close enough to where I can scoop him up in the net." To my surprise, that cricket actually turned and started swimming right toward me! I am telling you the truth; I was speechless! I didn't know they could even swim. I got him into the net and placed him over in the bushes where the dogs could not get to him.

As I walked back inside the house, shaking my head, I knew there was a lesson in this unbelievable story. Are you ready for it? You see, there are so many people we come across in this life who are struggling with one problem or another, holding on as best they can. Some of these people may not be to our liking and might be disgusting and dirty. But they are still drowning. They don't know if they will make it. Our simple acts of kindness may be the hope they need. When we share God's kindness with another, we may actually save that person. But for sure, we will help them see his loving kindness through us.

A little lame boy was once hurrying to catch a train. With people rushing every which way, he struggled to walk with his crutches, especially as he was carrying a basket full of fruit and candy. As the passengers pushed past him, one hit the basket by mistake, knocking oranges, apples, and candy bars in all directions. The man who caused the accident paused only long enough to scold the boy for getting in his way. Another gentleman, seeing the boy's distress, went to his aid. He quickly picked up the fruit and added a silver dollar to the collection, saying, "I'm sorry, Sonny! I hope this makes up a little!"

With a smile, the man was on his way. The boy had rarely seen such kindness. He called after the good Samaritan in gratitude and awe. "Mister—please, sir, are you Jesus?"

"No," replied the man gently. "I'm only one of his followers."

Every day, we meet people whose lives need to see the Lord in our acts of compassion and simple, thoughtful kindness. We just need to keep our eyes, ears, and hearts open.

What is this fruit of kindness all about anyway? The Greek word for kindness is *chrēstotēs*. It is not just kindness in our hearts but also kindness in our actions. It is the same kindness that our Father has for us every day.

Sadly, many people have ulterior, selfish motives when they help others. They may be seeking recognition or more likes on their YouTube channels. But godly kindness is just like God's kindness – it's selfless. The way you make someone feel is more powerful than what you say and even what you do. They will never forget those feelings. In our angry, chaotic, divisive culture, sometimes the only thing we can do as Christians is to show kindness in the way we treat others.

Overcoming evil with good does not come by human power; it comes only from the Holy Spirit's work in our lives. That means we need to stay in submission to the Holy Spirit's purpose. When we show the kindness of God, we are tender, thoughtful, and useful to others. Every action and every word will show grace to them, whether they are deserving or not. Sometimes it is even hard to show this attitude toward those we love, isn't it?

To express kindness toward strangers or toward those who oppose us requires the work of God on our hearts. That is why kindness is a fruit of the Spirit, because we must have the Spirit's help to show it to others. When we do it God's way, then our simple acts of kindness communicate: *I see you. I see your pain. And I believe you are worthy of love.* And isn't that just what he says to us all the time? We are all struggling humans, and when hard things disrupt our lives, we need a touch of kindness. It is a gift we give to others that draws them to him, not to us.

The opposite of kindness is not meanness, but rather selfishness. Sadly, we are living in a very selfish world. It is especially relevant in our society today because everywhere we turn, there is selfishness and a lack of grace. We see condemnation. We see judgment. It is everywhere—on the left, on the right, in our work, in our governments, in our schools, and even sometimes in our homes—there is a lack of grace. But that is not God's plan. He wants us to understand his grace and his loving kindness poured out on us. When we fully realize what he has done for us, it will be impossible to keep it to ourselves. His grace is contagious. We cannot help but give it away and express it to others.

King David understood about God's grace. His response to God's loving kindness? He shared it with someone unexpected—a young man named Mephibosheth. I know many parents-to-be love to choose Bible names for their babies—Paul, John, Peter, or the names of other disciples. Or maybe Old Testament names, such as Jacob, Joseph, or David. But why not name your baby boy Mephibosheth? It is a bit hard to pronounce, and he would probably have a difficult time learning to spell it in kindergarten, but it is definitely a memorable name.

Let's set the background of this story. Even though God was supposed to be the only king they would need, the Israelites wanted an earthly king to lead them into battle just like all the countries around them. God finally agreed, as long as the king would lead the people to stay faithful to him as their heavenly king. So, King Saul was their first earthly king. He was tall, dark, and handsome. He started out as a good king and led his troops into many successful battles against the surrounding kingdoms. But then Saul decided to take things into his own hands, doing things against God's commands. He started to lose his mind. You see, he was plagued by an evil spirit that often sent him into waves of madness. God had had enough and told Saul that he would be replaced as king. When Saul discovered that David was to be his successor, he tried to take David's life.

When you read the book of 1 Samuel, much of it talks about David hiding in caves and running for his life. Now, you would think that Saul's son, Jonathan, would hate David as well since it would have rightly been his kingdom after his father was replaced, not David's. But in reality, Jonathan and David became the best of friends. They were very close, and at one time, Jonathan even saved David's life and protected him from the wrath of his father, King Saul. In fact, they made a covenant with each other and promised that no matter what happened, they would always look after each other's families.

Now, Jonathan had a young son named Mirab Baal, which was a royal name, meaning "opponent of Baal" (a false pagan god). This little guy had a wonderful life in the palace. After all, his father was the prince, and his grandfather was the king. He had anything and everything a little boy could want. He even had his own nanny. But when Mirab Baal was only five years old, his life changed forever.

One day, a soldier came running into the palace and announced that both Jonathan and King Saul had been killed in battle. It sent the palace into a panic! I am sure there was a lot of crying and wailing and fear. Traditionally, when a king was killed or deposed, the new king would come in and destroy all of his predecessor's family, counselors, and servants. Can you imagine everyone running around, trying to escape? Little Mirab Baal was probably pretty confused. His nanny told him to run, and that is what he did. But since he was just a little boy, his small legs could not keep up. He just could not run fast enough! So, his nanny picked him up to carry him. That's when something happened. As she was running, she dropped Mirab Baal. The fall broke both of his feet. They couldn't just stop and go to the ER, so from that day on, he became crippled, never to walk again. Poor little guy! He lost his father and grandfather and became crippled all on the same day!

Now crippled and confused, Mirab Baal was taken to a desolate town called Lodebar, far away from the palace. You see, being part of the defeated royal family meant that he was also an enemy of the new king. The little guy's good name was even changed to Mephibosheth, which means son of shame. And so, for many years, he lived in Lodebar in secrecy, being cared for by others. He lived there in hiding, always looking over his shoulder, afraid he would be discovered.

Fast forward a few years, and David was thinking about his dear lost friend, Jonathan. He wondered, "Is there anyone still left of the house of Saul to whom I can show God's kindness for Jonathan's sake?" There was a servant of Saul's household named Ziba, so they summoned him to appear before David, and the king asked him the same question (2 Samuel 9:3, ESV). Ziba confessed, "Well, there is still a son of Jonathan; he is crippled in both feet." Then he told the king about Mephibosheth and where he was hiding. David ordered to have Mephibosheth brought to the palace immediately.

Can you imagine the scene? Mephibosheth was just hanging out at his home, all was good, and then one day, there was a knock at the door. *King David wants to see Mephibosheth!* Oh no! He had been found! I imagine there was some of that same panic he had felt as a little boy. What would the king want from him? He just knew that he would be killed, but he was ready to receive his sentence. When he arrived at the palace, he bowed before the king, prepared to face the music. But, instead, King David said, "Do not be afraid, for I will surely show you kindness for the sake of your father, Jonathan. I will restore to you all the land that belonged to your grandfather Saul, and you will always eat at my table" (2 Samuel 9:7, ESV).

Was he hearing this right? What did the king just tell him? Mephibosheth quickly put his face to the ground again and said, "What is your servant, that you should notice a dead dog like me?" (2 Samuel 9:8, ESV). But David did not change his mind! The king summoned Ziba and said to him, "I have given your master's grandson (Mephibosheth) everything that belonged to Saul and his family. You and your sons and your servants are to farm the land for him and bring in the crops, so that he may be provided for. And Mephibosheth will always eat at my table" (2 Samuel 9:9–10, NIV).

So, the story had a happy ending. Mephibosheth lived in Jerusalem, and he became like one of David's sons with the honor of always eating at the king's table. After all those years in hiding, King David had called for Mephibosheth, not to harm him, but to bless him. What a great story of kindness!

Do you see how much this is like the story of God's grace and kindness toward us? We are lost and crippled by our sins, aren't we? We may not be seeking the king, but he is seeking us! He calls us from the hopeless, desolate places in our lives and wants to redeem us, making us part of his family. Just like Mephibosheth, we have done nothing to deserve it. Our places of honor were provided by someone else, the Son of God himself. Someday, we, too, will sit at the banquet table of the king, not as servants, but as his royal children!

Praise God that his wonderful kindness toward us is never failing. With our utmost gratitude, we want to show his kindness to others, not because it will bring us recognition or make us feel good about ourselves, but because he has done so much for us. Today, the world still needs the Holy Spirit's fruit of kindness. People are hungry for the hope that they matter to someone—and they do. They matter to God and to us. He cares. And because he does, he lavishes his kindness on those who care about him and even on those who do not.

Acts 14:16–17 (ESV) explains, "In past generations he allowed all the nations to walk in their own ways. Yet he did not leave himself without witness, for he did good by giving you rains from heaven and fruitful seasons, satisfying your hearts with food and gladness." What a good God! For those who do not believe that he lives, and for those who do not even care if he does, our God still reaches out in kindness. And his kindness does not depend on the response of those he blesses; he is kind because that is who he is—a kindhearted God. We are called to show that same kindness through the Holy Spirit.

Millions of people will never open the Bible, but Christians are an open book to them, and we can open our lives by allowing his fruit of kindness to blossom, grow, and feed the hungry hearts of those we meet. Showing kindness is our way to show Christ to the world. Kindness flows from the heart. It is an action and reaction to the needs of others.

Your kindness may be what God uses to encourage someone when he or she feels like giving up. You may not even know a person is hurting. We all try to hide our hurts, don't we? When someone asks, we always say we are fine. So, ask God to guide you to that person who really needs you. It may be someone at work who seems fine but is in real pain. You may talk to someone online who puts up a good front, but he or she really needs someone to listen. You might meet a total stranger, and your smile or word of encouragement might make a big impact on his or her life.

You can be the difference between someone giving up or continuing to fight, between quitting or staying in the game, or even between feeling lost or finding real peace and hope. Just like I mentioned earlier, you need to keep your eyes, ears, and heart open.

Maybe you have been on the receiving end when someone showed God's kindness to you. Have you ever been at that place of despair when someone displayed godly thoughtfulness? I have! It was a time when Bill was out of work for more than two years. It was almost Christmas, and we did not know what we were going to do for gifts for our children. One day, Barb, a sweet lady from church, came by our house unannounced with bags full of wrapped gifts for all our family. It was so unexpected, but it was such a blessing. After all these years, I still remember that day. God had touched Barb's heart. She did not hesitate to share his kindness with us. Because of her kindness, we were reminded that God had not given up on us. We felt hopeful that he would see us through this struggle. It really made such a difference in our lives.

Watch and pray for practical ways to show kindness to others. The opportunities will be there! It is kindness and gratitude that move our hearts to buy the groceries of the lady who is struggling in line in front of us. It is a choice not to criticize but to help that single dad who is doing the best he can with three kids at Chick-fil-A.

Kindness is our response to hatred; it brings peace instead of conflict. Kindness is showing mercy instead of condemnation. It is compassion, which means to put yourself in the skin of another. That is exactly what God did for us in Christ. "The Word became flesh and made his dwelling among us" (John 1:14, NIV).

I know I have said it before, but we must be aware of the power we hold every single day: the power to be kind to everyone, especially to those who offer us nothing in return. When we intentionally choose to be kind, we will naturally become more joyful as well. It is a beautiful process—when you open your heart, your heart grows. You become more aware of the people around you, and you grow in understanding and compassion for them. It really does not matter how people respond or whether they pay back the kindness. It is simply showing the heart of Jesus to anyone you meet. That fruit of kindness is powerful and contagious!

Someone once said, "Kindness is giving hope to those who think they are all alone in the world." I have to add that it's also letting them *know* they are not alone in this world! Remember, it's not about you. To quote the great philosopher Jewel, "In the end, only kindness matters." So, instead of worrying about how to be pretty, just be pretty kind.

> *Grandma D.'s wisdom: I know that it's not always easy to be kind. But guess what: practice makes perfect! Start out with being kind in little ways. Even your family can use your kindness—maybe that might mean biting your tongue when they make mistakes or giving them unconditional love (and forgiveness) when they may not deserve it. Then ask God to open your eyes and your heart to serve those around you. Take up the challenge—who can I bless today? When you lay your head down on your pillow at night, you will feel good because your kindness made a difference in someone's life. I know you can do it!*
>
> *Love, Grandma D.*

Chapter 8

GOODNESS GRACIOUS!

Have you noticed how much we overuse the word *good* these days? That was a good burger! What a good movie! The concert was so good! We have really diluted the meaning of the word. All these uses are really just the opinion of the one who said them. You may think a certain burger is good, but I may not like all the toppings or how it was cooked. You may have enjoyed that movie, but it was too scary for me. What about that concert you went to? Everyone has different tastes in music. If I am not a fan of that particular genre, that would not be a "good" concert for me.

That reminds me of a time when my kids were watching a movie on television, and I needed to run over to the neighbor's house for a bit. I told them, "Be good!" They nodded as if they knew exactly what I was saying. When I got home, there was a mess all over the living room, and both kids were about to wrestle the other to the ground. I asked, "What is going on here? I told you to be good!" Their definition of being good was obviously different from mine. Their definition was simply that they would not kill one another! I learned quickly that moms must be very specific about every rule they expect their kids to follow. "Be good" just does not cover it! Maybe you'll figure that out more quickly than I did.

So, trying to pinpoint what God means when he wants us to have the fruit of goodness in our lives can also leave us scratching our heads. What does he mean for us to "be good?" The Bible tells us in Luke 18:19 that no one is good except God. In fact, it was Jesus himself who said this! Mark also recorded this surprising comment as well. In Mark

10:18 (NIV), Jesus says, "Why do you call me good? No one is good except God alone." Let me see if I understand this. No one is good except God, but Jesus tells me to be good? Well, if that is the case, it sounds impossible to achieve, doesn't it?

My goodness is not a checklist but a natural overflow of my gratitude to my Savior. It is manifested by the Holy Spirit's work in me. It goes hand in hand with the fruit of kindness. Most of us have a difficult time understanding the difference between the two. Kindness is how we treat people, and goodness is what we do for them. Goodness is kindness coming to life.

In Greek, the word goodness, *agathosune*, means "an uprightness of heart and life." It is only used in the Bible four times. In fact, it is not used outside of the Bible at all. *Agathos*, which means good, is used hundreds of times. (Know anyone named Agatha?) The word for kindness, on the other hand, is *chrestotes*. What is the difference between the two? With *agathosune* (goodness), we might need to rebuke and discipline if that is what is best for another person; but with *chrestotes* (kindness), we only help. Jesus is the best example. He showed *agathosune* when he cleansed the temple and drove out the moneychangers; but he also showed *chrestotes* when he was kind to the sinning woman who anointed his feet. Can you see the difference? We need that same kind of goodness that is both kind and strong.

I can learn to model goodness by first trying to understand God's goodness. I say "trying" because, just like his many other attributes, his goodness is beyond my human comprehension. Goodness is more than a trait; it is who he is. God *is* good!

It is because of God's goodness that he created this world in the first place. Genesis 1 tells us that God spoke into existence each part of creation. After each one, he saw that it was good. What does that mean? I think maybe God saw that all of creation met its intended function. Everything did what he planned for it to do. It accomplished its purpose and met his expectations. "And God saw that it was good" (Genesis 1:25, ESV). Likewise, that is one of the basic ideas of the goodness the Spirit wants to manifest in our lives—he wants us to fulfill our godly purposes as well.

God's goodness did not stop when he created the world. He created you and me! Each one of us is unique and totally loved by God. When he planned and created us, he gave us our special qualities and gifts to help us to fulfill his goodness in this world. Our purposes are to draw others to him by our good fruit. It is his goodness that we model with our lives when we serve others. It is what makes others drawn to him through us. Just like the rest of his creation, we are to accomplish the unique purpose he has for each of us. We meet those expectations when we model his character to others by what we do.

The true meaning of the word *goodness* is commonly overlooked. Goodness is action; it is not something we do only for the sake of being virtuous. Godly goodness is even more than that. It is a desire to honor, care for, and serve another person which, in turn, honors God. Is it easy? Definitely not when I try to do so on my own power! But God puts his goodness in us through the Holy Spirit. It is something that will continue to grow in us as we have more opportunities to do good to others.

One of my favorite stories in the Old Testament is the wonderful story of Ruth and Boaz. It shows the goodness and providence of God. The book of Ruth is a short book with only four chapters. But this story was a bright spot in the dismal, dark time of the Judges in Israel.

Here's a little background. There was a Jewish couple in the town of Bethlehem named Elimelech and his wife, Naomi. They had two sons, Mahlon and Chilion. There was a famine in Bethlehem, so the family packed up and headed to the foreign land of Moab. They lived there for several years, and after some time, Elimelech died. That left Naomi as a widow with two sons. The young men, going against the Jewish law, married two of the local girls, Orpah and Ruth. After about ten years, both Mahlon and Chilion also died, which made Naomi a poor widow without any sons to continue the family legacy.

Naomi knew that being a poor widow was not an easy life, and on top of that, she was a foreigner in Moab. She heard that the famine was over in Bethlehem, so she decided to go back home to be near her family. She told her daughters-in-law to think about their future and go back to their families because she was leaving Moab. They all hugged each other and cried. Orpah went back to her Mom and Dad, but Ruth had something to say to Naomi.

Then we have the beautiful words of Ruth that I just love: "Do not urge me to leave you or to return from following you. For where you go, I will go, and where you lodge, I will lodge. Your people shall be my people, and your God my God. Where you die, I will die, and there will I be buried. May the Lord do so to me and more also if anything but death parts me from you" (Ruth 1:16–17, ESV). That sure tugs at my heartstrings! Ruth loved Naomi so much that she was willing to move away from her family, her culture, and her god. She told Naomi that she wanted Yahweh to be her God as well. That really tells us so much about the kind of relationship they had, doesn't it?

So, they headed back to Bethlehem together—a poor Jewish widow and a young Moabite widow. The Israelites did not like the Moabites, so Ruth was going to a foreign land where she would not only be lonely, but also an unwelcome refugee.

Naomi and Ruth made it safely to Bethlehem. Naomi was so depressed and miserable. She even blamed God for the deaths of her husband and sons. She told everyone to just call her Mara, which means bitterness. Ruth still loved Naomi even when she was grumpy. She went into the fields to glean leftover grain behind the reapers so they would have something to eat. You see, God had a kind of "welfare system" in place that allowed the poor to pick up leftover grain after the workers finished harvesting. That way, even the poor would not go hungry (Leviticus 23:22).

One day, when Ruth was gleaning grain, she "happened" to glean in the field of Boaz, a wealthy man who was a relative of Naomi's late husband, Elimelech. One day, Boaz was out walking through his fields and saw this gorgeous young woman picking up grain. He called the foreman over to ask who this lovely lady belonged to. The foreman explained that she was Ruth, the young Moabite woman who came back with Naomi. He said she had asked permission to glean in the field and had been working there all day since early morning.

Boaz eagerly went over to meet the lovely Ruth, and his heart beat faster (in my romantic thinking anyway). Not only was she beautiful, but she was polite, humble, hard-working, and good to her mother-in-law. Boaz told her to only glean in his field, drink water from his vessels, and stay with his young women as they were working. He wanted to protect her and keep her safe, so he told all his young men not to touch her. Ruth was so appreciative of Boaz's goodness, she fell down on her face and asked him, "Why have I found favor in your eyes, that you should notice me? I'm a foreigner" (Ruth 2:10, NIV). Boaz smiled and told her that everyone was talking about all that Ruth had been doing for Naomi, and about how she left her family and her land to come to a land that she did not know. It was her goodness to Naomi that prompted Boaz to be good to her. He even invited her to dine with him and told his workers to "accidentally" drop some of the bundles of grain for her to pick up. What a good guy!

When Ruth got home, she told Naomi what happened and all that Boaz had told her. Then Naomi hatched a plan. She explained to Ruth that Boaz was a relative and a "kinsman-redeemer." Now this kinsman-redeemer thing is pretty complicated. In Old Testament Jewish families, wealth was passed down from male to male, never to women. If a husband died, the kinsman-redeemer would take care of the widow and provide for her. If she had no male heirs, then the kinsman-redeemer would marry her and have a son with her to keep the property and wealth in her family, and to keep the deceased man's lineage going. The deceased man's wealth would be the legacy of the son of the kinsman-redeemer and widow. The kinsman-redeemer would get nothing out of this deal—well, maybe except the honor of doing the right thing. Pretty confusing, isn't it?

Back to Naomi's plan. It certainly was not a wise one! What was she thinking? She took matters into her own hands rather than waiting on Boaz to act on his feelings or, more importantly, for God to make things happen his way. She told Ruth to get all dressed up in her prettiest dress, put on some sweet-smelling perfume, and make herself irresistible. She instructed Ruth that after Boaz finished eating, got drunk, and fell asleep, she should climb into bed with him. That was quite a risky plan! Ruth did just what Naomi told her. She sneaked into the room where Boaz was sleeping and quietly got into his bed, lying at his feet. (This is a good example of how God can even use our "messes" for his glory!)

About midnight, Boaz woke up and was startled to see a woman lying in his bed. "Who are you?" he asked. Ruth told him who she was and pretty much proposed to him, "Spread your wings over your servant, for you are my redeemer" (Ruth 3:9, ESV). This is where the plan could have really backfired. Thankfully, Boaz was a good and moral man. He told Ruth that he was honored by her request, but that there was another man who was a closer relative and who could be her kinsman-redeemer. He could have easily taken advantage of her, but instead, he told her to go to sleep. He would keep her safe and take care of everything in the morning. Boaz kept his faith in God and honored Ruth at the same time. Early the next morning, he discretely sent Ruth back to Naomi before anyone could gossip about her.

Boaz then went to the town gate, which is where the Jewish men always conducted business. With ten of the elders as witnesses, he met with the other relative of Elimelech who had "first dibs" on buying Naomi's land and marrying Ruth. Boaz was kind of sneaky. He told the man that he was the closest kinsman-redeemer, not Boaz, so he needed to decide if he wanted to buy the land. He eagerly agreed. But then Boaz told him that when he bought the land, part of the deal is that he would have to marry the Moabite woman, Ruth. You know, the Moabite woman from the terrible land of Moab? The other man shook his head and quickly backed out of the deal. So, Boaz officially become Ruth's redeemer. They got married and lived happily ever after (that's my fairytale ending, anyway).

Here's the best part of this story: because Boaz redeemed Ruth, they had a baby born in Bethlehem named Obed, who became the ancestor of a baby born in Bethlehem named Jesus, our Messiah! Boaz's act of redemption brought about the redemption of the whole world!

If you think about it, Ruth's choice to stay with Naomi was one of the most decisive moments in all of world history. It started a chain of events that can be explained only by the hand of God—a famine, a family moving to a foreign land, a young man marrying a woman not of his culture, the deaths of a woman's husband and sons, a sad trip back to her homeland, a young immigrant gleaning in a certain field at a certain time, and the goodness of a godly man to a foreigner. All these events lead to the birth of our Messiah, twenty-seven generations later! It gives me goosebumps!

Just like Boaz, when we act out of the true goodness of our hearts, we do what is best for others. Those actions can only come from a relationship with God and from a place of selflessness. We place the needs of others before our own.

Of course, the life of Jesus Christ is the perfect example of goodness. He thought of our needs even when it meant incredible pain for him. He selflessly chose to die a horrible death on the cross for the sins of humanity and to give us the gift of eternal life. His ministry of sacrifice is an example of God's goodness toward all of us. After all, the term *gospel* means "good news."

Just like the fruit in God's spiritual garden, goodness needs to be cultivated. I can be called a good person by others, but if my life does not model the ultimate goodness of the Father, my purpose is not what he expects of me. A Spirit-filled life is more than just doing nice things; it is working to do what is best for others. Am I watching for ways to serve, encourage, and exhort? How can I draw another person closer to him by what they see in me?

When tragedy strikes, there are so many people, Christians and non-Christians, willing to serve and help. Think about all the volunteers who show up after a tornado or hurricane, or the ones who help after a family has a house fire. There are many people who are on the spot offering money, items, and food, or even physical labor. These are all wonderful acts of service. But what is the difference between this kind of goodness versus Spirit-filled goodness? There is a difference—holy goodness goes beyond the needs of the moment and focuses on the needs of the heart. It causes me to serve immediately but to do more than that. What can I do for this person that will let them see God? How can my actions draw this person into a deeper relationship with him? Will my actions confirm to them how much he loves them? Will they see the Father or just me? True goodness makes me get out of my own way!

I have had so much goodness shown to me over the years. My Christian sisters have taken my hand when times were tough. When my husband Bill had two difficult brain surgeries and was out of work for two years, they continued helping us in so many ways. We never missed a car or house payment; our children were cared for; we even had gifts for Christmas and birthdays. Meals, cards, and phone calls were constant reminders that they cared for us. I knew that God himself was ministering to us through them. When Bill died a few years later, these Christian sisters served and kept on serving months after my worldly friends had gone away. It amazes me to think of all the ways they put my needs before their own, even doing the dirty work of cleaning my house, doing my laundry, preparing meals, and caring for my family. It went so far beyond those physical needs, however. They sat beside me, held my hand, hugged me as I cried, and listened to me over and over. They encouraged me, prayed with me, and guided me through the darkness. Their Spirit-filled goodness was overflowing; it was tenacious and determined. I knew that their love for God motivated them even when their physical bodies wanted to quit. God used them to carry me through months of grief.

God knows that this world can be pretty tough on many of his children. Ask God to open your eyes and see others as he sees them. It might be a friend who needs you, but it also may be a stranger. It may be that mom with small children struggling in the Walmart parking lot. It may be that older woman standing at the bus stop with a heavy bag full of all her possessions. It may even be that friend of your own son or daughter who hangs out at your house playing video games.

Jesus told his followers a parable about what goodness really means to him. In Matthew 25:31–40, he talked about the judgment day and how the sheep (righteous) and the goats (the unrighteous) would be divided. He named several acts of service that the righteous had done for the king. They were confused and asked him, "Lord, when did we see you hungry and feed you, or thirsty and give you something to drink? When did we see you a stranger and invite you in, or needing clothes and clothe you? When did we see you sick or in prison and go to visit you?" The king replied, "I tell you the truth, whatever you did for one of the *least of these brothers of mine*, you did for me" (verses thirty-seven to forty, NIV).

Our Father isn't concerned about us "converting" others to him. He is concerned about us loving people by being good to them. He wants us to be his hands and feet to this lost world. The more we cultivate godly goodness, the more our servant hearts will grow. Others will see Jesus living in us and will want to know more about this God we serve. They will see something in our lives that they are missing in theirs. It may be our confidence, our joy, our peace, or our hope. Someone has said, "I'd rather see a sermon than hear one any day." We don't have to push anything down their throats. We just need to be gracious as we serve, minister, and love others. Now, understand this—if we try to do this on our own, it won't work. It will only happen when we yield to the power of the Holy Spirit living in us.

People always speak of a life of comfort and affluence as "the good life." But living a life close to God with all the great benefits God offers is truly the good life! It is a life that so many know nothing about but so desperately need! When we allow God to cultivate in us the fruit of goodness, it will lead us to the gift of eternal life. And that, my friend, is as good as it gets!

> *Grandma D.'s wisdom: Honestly, it's really not important to know the difference between kindness and goodness. Just keep your eyes and your heart open to the needs of those around you and serve them. Think about what your life would be like without the love of your heavenly Father. Oh my, how empty and sad it would be. That is just how others are feeling, hoping for someone to show them a little care. God wants that someone to be you! Don't be nervous. I know you can do it.*
>
> *Love, Grandma D.*

Chapter 9

FAITHFUL IN THE FIRE!

There is a story about a terrible drought that hit a rural farm community in Kansas many years ago. Farmers were worried about their crops, which affected everyone in the community. Encouraged by their local preacher, they all decided to meet at the community church to pray together and ask God to send much-needed rain. When the day arrived, everyone showed up ready to pray. One little boy brought an umbrella with him. Everyone smiled, giggled, and shook their heads. You see, everyone came ready to pray, but only one small boy came ready to see God answer. That is faith!

The Bible talks about us having faith the size of a tiny mustard seed. That doesn't sound like much, does it? I think I have at least that little bit. Don't you? Jesus told his followers in Matthew 17:20 (NIV), "Truly I tell you, if you have faith as small as a mustard seed, you can say to this mountain, 'Move from here to there,' and it will move. Nothing will be impossible for you." So, how can that itty-bitty faith move mountains? I believe faith must be something deeper than we think.

When I first thought about the fruit of faithfulness, I just knew this would be the easiest chapter to write. After all, I am a Christian, and faith is a part of my life every day. However, the more I have studied, the more I have realized that faithfulness is more encompassing than I ever understood. The faithfulness of God is undeniable. It is constant and unwavering. If I believe that my faithfulness needs to mirror his, then I will be a person of faith despite my circumstances. Whoa! Now we are getting into some tough stuff! Faith, even when life is falling apart, seems impossible, doesn't it?

What is faithfulness? Is it more than believing in God? Absolutely! There are several definitions of faithful in the dictionary—it means trustworthy, dependable, steadfast, unswerving, keeping your word. How beautifully these words describe our Father! In fact, the Bible compares him to a faithful bridegroom.

We've all seen that bridegroom waiting at the altar to get a glimpse of his beautiful bride. With tears in his eyes, he smiles as she walks toward him. He is so full of love, and he doesn't hesitate to say, "I'm all in!" God is like that—he is totally committed and faithful to his covenant with us, his bride. We can rest on his promises! Every one of them is trustworthy!

I understand that some of us come from difficult backgrounds. You may have been abused. You may have been lied to by your parents. Your spouse may have forgotten those until-death-do-us-part vows and walked away. Others may have told you what you so desperately wanted to hear, but you knew they would not keep their word. Sometimes being hurt and lied to repeatedly can spill over into our trust in God. Isn't he just someone else who is going to let us down? After all these other disappointments, we prepare ourselves for the worst. We refuse to be a victim again.

So, before we talk about our faithfulness, let's look at our Father's faithfulness toward us. As we see examples of his unwavering dependability, we can put our trust in him. The Bible is filled with hundreds of promises from our heavenly Father, promises that we can lean on no matter what our circumstances may be. We can rest assured that he is faithful to fulfill every one of them. As you read Bible verses about the promises of God, claim them for your life! Whatever you need, he has a promise for it! It may be freedom from addiction; overcoming sin; financial provision; hope for lost and hurting family members; recovering your marriage; good health; being free from fear, anxiety, and depression; or strength. The list goes on and on. There are so many blessings and gifts that God promises us as his children. Here are a few of my favorites:

God loves us unconditionally! "For I am convinced that neither death nor life, neither angels nor demons, neither the present nor the future, nor any powers, neither height nor depth, nor anything else in all creation, will be able to separate us from the love of God that is in Jesus Christ our Lord" (Romans 8:38–39, NIV).

God will protect us! "Fear not, for I am with you; be not dismayed, for I am your God; I will strengthen you, I will help you, I will uphold you with my righteous right hand" (Isaiah 41:10 ESV). "Even though I walk through the valley of the shadow of death, I will fear no evil, for you are with me; your rod and your staff, they comfort me" (Psalm 23:4, ESV).

God is always with us! "Have I not commanded you? Be strong and courageous! Do not tremble or be dismayed, for the Lord your God is with you wherever you go" (Joshua 1:9, ESV).

God is our safe place, our rest! "He who dwells in the shelter of the Most High will rest in the shadow of the Almighty. I will say of the Lord, he is my refuge and my fortress, my God, in whom I trust" (Psalm 91:1–2, NIV).

God will never abandon us! "It is the Lord who goes before you. He will be with you. He will not leave you or forsake you. Do not fear or be dismayed" (Deuteronomy 31:8, ESV).

God's love is unending, unfailing, and unchanging! "Though the mountains be shaken, and the hills be removed, yet my unfailing love for you will not be shaken, nor my covenant of peace be removed, says the Lord, who has compassion on you" (Isaiah 54:10, NIV).

God hears our prayers! "The righteous cry out, and the Lord hears them; he delivers them from all their troubles. The Lord is close to the brokenhearted and saves those crushed in spirit" (Psalm 34:17–18 NIV). "And this is the confidence that we have toward him, that if we ask anything according to his will he hears us" (1 John 5:14, ESV).

God is faithful to us! "He who calls you is faithful; he will surely do it" (1 Thessalonians 5:24 ESV). "The Lord is faithful. He will establish you and guard you against the evil one" (2 Thessalonians 3:3, ESV).

God has a home for us in heaven with him! "Let not your hearts be troubled. Believe in God; believe also in me. In my Father's house are many rooms. If it were not so, would I have told you that I go to prepare a place for you? And if I go and prepare a place for you, I will come again and will take you to myself, that where I am you may be also" (John 14:1–3, ESV).

What comfort and encouragement we find in these promises! There are so many more promises of God in his Word. In every single one of them, he reminds us that he is always faithful. So, how can I, in turn, be faithful to him? How can I show my gratitude to him and my confidence that he is the only one in whom my hope lies?

As we read the story of the children of Israel, it is filled with their wishy-washy faith. I can't help but shake my head every time I read about their grumbling and complaining. Many times, this happened right after God has just shown them his love and protection in miraculous ways. How quickly they would forget!

When God finally had enough of their unfaithfulness and worshipping false gods, he allowed the Babylonians to capture and enslave them. The king of Babylon at this time was a guy named Nebuchadnezzar. Now, after he captured the Israelites, he decided that he wanted the best-looking, brightest, strongest, and smartest of the young men to be taught the language and literature of his culture. He even gave them all new names.

These young men included four we are familiar with—Daniel and his friends, Shadrach, Meshach, and Abednego. God was with these four young men, and they grew in their learning and skill beyond what anyone else had. Eventually, the king made them royalty, no longer slaves. Now, there are some parts of this story concerning food and dreams that you can read for yourself in the first couple of chapters of Daniel. What happened after that is when it gets really interesting.

King Nebuchadnezzar decided to build a golden image more than ninety-eight feet high and had it placed in the center of his kingdom. He commanded that when the people of every nation and language heard the band of instruments playing music, they were to fall down and worship—not God, but the image that the king had built. If they did not do so, they would immediately be thrown into a burning, fiery furnace. Seriously, that would have been an easy thing to fake. Fall on your face and just *pretend* you were worshipping the image, right? Just go with the flow. Don't rock the boat. But for Shadrach, Meshach, and Abednego, that was not even a consideration. They refused to follow the king's order.

It turns out there were some jealous tattletales in the kingdom.

They told King Nebuchadnezzar that some of the Israelites he had appointed over the affairs of Babylon were ignoring the king's orders. It probably would have been pretty obvious, because when the music started, everyone fell flat on their faces. Here were three guys still upright, not hiding, but standing defiantly and ignoring the order.

The king was furious and ordered that Shadrach, Meshach, and Abednego be brought to him. He asked them if what he had heard was true. He wanted to give them another chance. He basically told them, okay, guys, maybe you didn't understand. I'll give you a do-over. When you hear the instruments start to play, fall down and worship the image, and all will be good. No biggie, just fall down. He looked at them and warned them once more. "If you do not bow down and worship it, you will be thrown immediately into the blazing furnace!" Then he added this challenge: "After all, what god can rescue you out of my hand?" (Daniel 3:15, NIV). That last statement was a big mistake, Nebuchadnezzar!

Then, in Daniel 3:16–18 (NLT), the three young men looked the king in the eye and answered: "O Nebuchadnezzar, we do not need to defend ourselves before you. If we are thrown into the blazing furnace, the God whom we serve is able to save us. He will rescue us from your power, Your Majesty. But even if he doesn't, we want to make it clear to you, Your Majesty, that we will never serve your gods or worship the gold statue you have set up." In other words, they were bravely saying that they served a God who is faithful, and they would be faithful to him no matter what.

The king become furious with Shadrach, Meshach, and Abednego, who disobeyed even after he had given them a second chance. It was as if they had mocked him, and that was unacceptable. Nebuchadnezzar had the young men bound up, wearing their coats, tunics, hats, and other garments. Then he ordered the furnace to be heated seven times hotter than it normally was. The soldiers who bound the young men opened the furnace door, and because it was so hot, the fire killed them all just like that. So, just picture Shadrach, Meshach, and Abednego tied up and standing there in front of the door with dead soldiers around them. They were not pushed in the flames; they fell in. I imagine they looked at each other, shrugged their shoulders, and just leaned forward to fall into the furnace.

When Nebuchadnezzar looked into the furnace, he was flabbergasted. He asked his counselors, "I thought we put three men into the furnace, but I see four men. They are unbound, walking around, and not hurt. And the fourth one looks like the son of the gods!" (Daniel 3:25, NIV). This is one of those rare Old Testament moments where I believe Christ himself shows up. I would love to know what the four of them talked about in that furnace!

So, Nebuchadnezzar shouted, "Shadrach, Meshach, and Abednego, servants of the Most-High God, come out here!" (3:26). They came out of the furnace, and all the king's counselors and servants gathered around to look at them. They saw that not even a hair on their heads was singed, their clothes were clean and unharmed, and they did not even smell like smoke—which can be pretty strong.

How did Nebuchadnezzar respond to this? At the end of Daniel 3, he said, "Praise be to the God of Shadrach, Meshach, and Abednego, who has sent his angel and rescued his servants. They trusted in him and defied the king's command and were willing to give up their lives rather than serve any god except their own God" (Daniel 3:28, NIV). The king was not done. He made a decree that if anyone said anything against the God of Shadrach, Meshach, and Abednego, they would be torn limb from limb and their houses destroyed.

By the next chapter, King Nebuchadnezzar was praising God and telling everyone about his mighty signs and wonders. He realized that God Almighty was the true God, and that he was not. God humbled Nebuchadnezzar in a mighty way. But he did so by him witnessing the faithful, unswerving trust and loyalty of three young men who chose not to take the easy way out. In turn, because of these three men, Nebuchadnezzar witnessed the faithfulness of God. And his life was drastically changed!

Let's back up in this story a bit to the faith of those three young men and their testimony before the king. Their words were sure and confident. They knew without a doubt that their God was always faithful. He was truly in charge, not King Nebuchadnezzar. I want you to look more closely at that phrase, "but even if he doesn't." It is pretty powerful. Say, for example, you just got some bad news from your doctor: you have stage 4 cancer. There is nothing they can do. You are faced with a choice. You still believe that God can heal you. You have seen him do so before. Do you doubt, or do you hang on to him believing that he knows best? "But even if he doesn't …"

Because of the pandemic, you and your husband both lost your jobs. Now your finances have taken a nosedive. You do not know how you will pay your bills. It is overwhelming. You know that God promises to take care of his children. You know he can put his hand into this mess and put others in your life to help you. "But even if he doesn't …"

You might be in the middle of some serious family problem, maybe with your spouse or your kids. You are praying constantly for God to step in and help. You know God wants your family to be whole. You trust him and ask him to make it all right again. "But even if he doesn't …"

"But even if he doesn't …" That is a powerful statement of faith, isn't it? We know that our Father is faithful, and we trust his word. We have a choice to believe in him or not. We know that his love for us is perfect, and he will do what is best, even if it is not what we want. So, even if the choice to trust is a difficult one, we will remain faithful, *no matter what*!

But let's get real. Some things in life really stink. Some days it is hard to get out of bed and put one foot in front of the other. The pain can be physical, emotional, or spiritual. Disappointment can overwhelm us. What lies ahead can panic us. There might be loneliness, pain, sadness, anger, fear, and even an unexplainable sense of dread. We all have had struggles of some kind, some so serious we cannot imagine one more day. I do not want to minimize that or sugarcoat it. There have been times when I have fallen, face-down on the floor, sobbing until there were no tears left. Why, Lord? When we feel we are at the end of our strength, sometimes all we can do is hang on to the only one who is our strength. Even when we can't understand or can't see his plan, all we can do is trust his heart. His love and care for you are unwavering. Hang on to that!

Several years ago, I was in a dark place in my life. I wondered if God even cared about me. My husband's frequent seizures were so severe and stressful. They not only caused him to have terrible side effects, but also to sometimes become violent. It was scary, and I felt all alone. I wrestled with how to protect myself and my children and yet stay faithful to my marriage vows. When Bill wasn't having a seizure, everything was okay.

One day, I went to my regular family doctor for a sore throat. Dr. Maxwell had been my doctor for several years, so he knew me pretty well. During my visit, he asked me how I was doing. I told him I had a sore throat. After he examined me, he asked, "How are you really doing?" He knew about Bill's seizures, so I said, "It's not easy." He asked about my prayer life, which surprised me. I said, with tears in my eyes, "If it wasn't for my faith in God, I don't know what I would do." Then he pulled out his prescription pad and wrote me a prescription. I thought it was an antibiotic for an ear infection or maybe a sedative since I was boo-hooing in his office. But it wasn't like any other prescription I have ever received. It said, "When the Night Is Falling" by Dennis Jernigan. I looked at him, and he said, "I want you to go and buy this CD. Then put your headphones on, lie down on your bed or even on the floor, and play this over and over. It will remind you how much God loves you. Play it until you believe it!" Pretty amazing advice from a doctor, isn't it?

I did what he said and bought the CD. I put my headphones on and laid down on the floor. As I listened to the lyrics of that song, I cried and cried. I played it again and again, and I soon felt a peace and comfort I had not known in quite a long time. It was amazing to think that God loves me so much that he sings over me! Zephaniah 3:17 (NIV) says, "The LORD your God is with you, the Mighty Warrior who saves. He will take great delight in you; in his love he will no longer rebuke you, but he will rejoice over you with singing."

By the way, Dr. Maxwell is still my doctor and one of my favorite people! God used him to remind me just how precious and loved I am! I had the opportunity to meet Dennis Jernigan a few months later. I told him about this unusual prescription and how it helped me to heal. He was so touched and shared the story with others he met.

Maybe you need reminding like I did that your heavenly Father is deeply and completely in love with you. When the darkness hides your way, or when you wonder how you can take one more step, remember he is singing over you, too. What is he singing? I'm sure it's these simple words—*Oh, how I love you, my child!* Just hang on and keep listening. Here are some of the lyrics to Dennis's song:

When the Night Is Falling

When the night is falling
And the day is done,
I can hear you calling, "Come."
I will come, while you sing over me.
When the night surrounds me,
All my dreams undone,
I can hear you calling, "Come."
I will come, while you sing over me.
(Dennis Jernigan, 1989)

If you are struggling, you may find comfort in music as well. Reading through the Psalms, which are so full of pain and despair and God's healing hand, can also be helpful. Remember, your faith—even when it is weak and worn—is all he asks. His faithfulness is enough.

Here is what I want you to remember: *The God we serve is a faithful God!* You may have to go through the fire, but you will never have to go through it alone. He will not send you through sickness or relationship struggles or financial problems or any other kind of struggles without him going through them with you. "Who is that fourth guy in there?" It is the Son of God, and he is walking with you. Be faithful to him; follow his lead. He is always faithful, and he is with you in the fire.

Grandma D.'s wisdom: Hey, sweet one, how are you really doing today? Are you feeling overwhelmed, lost, scared, hopeless? I'm so sorry. I wish I could take away your pain and make the bad things go away. As difficult as it may be, keep believing that your Father truly loves you and will never leave you. He will give you strength even at your darkest moments. I'm praying that you can feel his presence. Just fall into his open arms. He's got you! Great is his faithfulness!

Love, Grandma D.

Chapter 10

GENTLE AS A ... CHICKEN?

The last thing I would ever think about when considering the fruit of gentleness is a chicken! They are noisy and messy. But many years ago, my mama told me a story that changed my thinking a bit.

Mama grew up on a farm in the 1940s. Her family was poor, so everyone had to help out on the farm. One of her chores was to take care of the chickens. Every day before school, she had to feed them and gather the eggs. She loved watching the baby chicks waddling after their mothers and peeping constantly. Mother hens were protective of their babies. They chirped warnings when the chicks would start to wander off. They gathered them together under their wings when danger was coming.

One spring evening there was an intense, scary storm—torrents of heavy rain, strong whipping winds, booming thunder shaking the ground, and flashes of lightening that brightened the sky like daylight. One lightning bolt crashed into the barn and caught it on fire. The family was able to save the animals, but the barn was a total loss. The next day, sadly, they found a mother hen that had perished in the fire. Under her wings were four baby chicks still alive and safe. That mama had protected her babies with her own life!

I think about that story every time I read Matthew 23:37. Jesus was the perfect definition of true gentleness. Even after he rebuked the scribes and Pharisees, Jesus showed gentleness and how he felt even about those who opposed him. He lamented: "O Jerusalem, Jerusalem, the one who kills the prophets and stones those who are sent to her!

How often I wanted to gather your children together, as a hen gathers her chicks under her wings, but you were not willing!" (NKJV).

We have already talked about love, joy, peace, patience, kindness, goodness, and faithfulness. Now, we come to gentleness. The world tells us that being gentle just means you are weak and wimpy. That is certainly not something we want to strive for. It does not sound like something the Holy Spirit would want to cultivate in us either. After all, the fruit of the Spirit makes us more like our heavenly Father, and he is certainly not weak or wimpy! If we behaved that way, I don't think those characteristics are ones that would draw others to him. And that is our purpose in showing his fruit in our lives.

There are many different meanings for gentleness. The dictionary defines it as "the quality of being kind, tender, or mild-mannered." Strong's Greek Concordance says that the word "refers to exercising God's strength under His control … demonstrating power without undue harshness … gentleness (reserve) and strength." The closest English word is probably graciousness. We are gracious, considerate, humble, calm, and others-focused when we are gentle. It is a tender, compassionate approach toward others' weaknesses and limitations. Reserve and strength. Power and control. These are not words that come to mind when we think of gentleness, are they?

Sometimes I wish I could have hung out with Jesus, maybe gone fishing with him, and then sit by a campfire while he cooked fish (that he had created). Then I could experience firsthand his gentleness that was never ever weakness at all. It is what Jesus modeled for us, and it is the way our Father wants us to act toward others, even those we may not agree with or those we see as undeserving.

Throughout his ministry, Jesus did the opposite of what everyone else did. He ate with the outcasts, healed the sick, and wept at his friend Lazarus's death. Even though he was the Son of God, we are amazed by his humility as he let women anoint him with expensive perfume and as he tied a towel around his waist and washed his disciples' feet.

What did Jesus do when he saw the unclean? What was his response when he came across prostitutes and lepers? He had pity on them and knew that they longed for compassion. He moved toward them, not away. He spent time with them. He touched them. When Jesus, who was perfect and clean, touched an unclean sinner, Jesus did not become unclean as the Jewish law stipulated. Instead, the sinner became clean. He gave humanity back to those the world saw as undeserving.

In Matthew 11:29 (ESV), Christ said, "Take my yoke upon you and learn from me, for I am *gentle* and lowly in heart, and you will find rest for your souls." Jesus showed us that strength and gentleness can live together in our lives. His demonstration of gentleness was the ultimate example of strength.

When you think about the apostle Paul, do you ever think about him being gentle? Brave, yes. Bold, yes. Faithful, yes. Determined, yes. But gentle? Well, not really. In 1 Thessalonians 2:7 (ESV), he gives us a glimpse of how he treated others: "We were gentle among you, like a nursing mother taking care of her own children." Paul knew that for others to see Jesus in him, he had to treat them with the same gentleness that Jesus showed him. He knew that gentleness is a strong hand with a soft touch.

It is not always easy for us, is it? When we are angry or frustrated, we have the strength without the gentleness. No one can make you mad. Anger is a choice. You can choose to be offended or not. A gentle person chooses his or her attitudes and reactions based on pleasing God instead of reacting to people. It is how we choose to deal with the mistakes, failures, and weaknesses of others. You would want them to show that same gentleness toward you, wouldn't you?

Gentleness is being submissive to God rather than being controlled by others. It is a measure of God's identity as he uses us to gently touch a wounded world. As a fruit of the Spirit, it is nothing less than power under control—but God's power, not ours! Just like a mature apple tree produces apples, a mature Christian produces gentleness. But it is only with the help of the Holy Spirit in our lives that we can be gentle even when it seems impossible.

This world is in utter chaos. Sin and evil are everywhere. Our climate is one of conflict, anger, and unrest. It seems to get worse all the time, doesn't it? By our gentleness, we can show others that violent encounters and situations ruled by emotion are not the answer. When we demonstrate gentleness, even when we might be provoked, we are showing others that there is a better way to live. God's purpose is for us to demonstrate gentleness to change their lives and draw them into a relationship with him. The apostle Paul told the Philippians, "Let your gentleness be evident to all. For the Lord is near" (Philippians 4:5, NIV).

How do we make our gentleness evident and visible to others? When conflicts arise, we must not be harsh or judgmental, but instead we must be slow to become angry. We are not only to be aware of what we say, but how we say it. If someone treats us wrongly and hurts us, we could easily get upset and break the relationship. But with gentleness, we look at the person's heart and give him or her the benefit of the doubt. We assume the best about him or her rather than the worst. We are God-controlled rather than others-controlled.

Did you notice those two potent, challenging words in that Philippians 4:5 verse? Paul said, "to *all*." Our gentleness is not just shown to those easy-to-get-along-with people, but to *all*! That includes those who give and those who take. It includes the person who gets your order wrong and the mechanic who does not fix the problem with your car. It includes the people who cut you off in traffic and the moms who don't go through the pick-up line the right way at school. How gentle were you with them? It includes those people who are not like us, those people who do not like us, and those people who disagree with us (including politically). It includes those who frustrate us and those who repeatedly fail or disappoint us, like our families.

Sometimes we are the least gentle with our children and spouses. That is just sad! Not only are we to show gentleness to our children, but we are to teach them how God is gentle, loving, and forgiving of them. As they see gentleness modeled in us, they will want more of it in their lives and, in turn, they will model gentleness to others.

I like to compare the perfect picture of gentleness as to how you would hold a tiny infant. When a new mother cautiously hands you her sweet little baby, you treat that little one as fragile and breakable. You are soft and sweet-talking. You gently hold the child close and give him or her all your careful, loving attention. You do not think about what you want; your attention is not on yourself. All your concern and focus is on taking care of that baby. You want to keep the child safe and protected. You would do anything to keep the baby from harm.

That is how we should treat others—with the same gentle, loving care that you would give that baby. When you are gentle with someone, you are tender and would not hurt them even though you could. You choose not to exercise strength but rather show protective care. Your words are soft and thoughtful. So, hold on to relationships like you hold on to a baby. That means you do whatever it takes to keep someone from being harmed.

John the Baptist referred to Jesus's humility and gentleness by calling him "the Lamb." In Old Testament times, the sacrifice of a spotless lamb was needed for the atonement of the sins of Israel. That lamb did not just hop on the alter. It had to be caught and carried, wiggling all the way, and then held down to prepare it for the sacrifice. But Jesus, in his humility and gentleness, *willingly* became that Lamb for us to take away our sins and give us eternal life. He loved us that much! "Behold the Lamb of God who takes away the sins of the world" (John 1:29, ESV).

In Old Testament prophecies as well as the New Testament accounts of Jesus's ministry, his focus was on others to the sacrifice of his own needs, and he patiently endured all the wrongs inflicted on him.

There is also so much imagery of Jesus as a gentle, loving shepherd. Isaiah talked about Jesus coming with might, but he contrasted that with this beautiful image in Isaiah 40:11 (ESV): "He will tend his flock like a shepherd; he will gather the lambs in his arms; he will carry them in his bosom, and gently lead those that are with young."

The most perplexing part of his gentleness and humility is that he became a human—a helpless newborn baby—for you and me! He could have just gone *poof* and appeared as a man, but he became a tiny infant, totally dependent on humans, the very ones he came to save. It was his choice to leave the perfection of heaven and the presence of God to draw us to him. "He emptied himself, by taking the form of a servant, being born in the likeness of men. And being found in human form, he humbled himself by becoming obedient to the point of death, even death on a cross" (Philippians 2:7–9, ESV).

Of course, it is easy to be gentle when we are around those we care for and who care about us in return. But to do the same for strangers or for people who hurt us? That is extremely challenging! But that is just what Jesus did. Even on the cross, Jesus was gentle and merciful with those who were crucifying him. "Father, forgive them for they do not know what they are doing" (Luke 23:34, ESV). It amazes me how our Savior could forgive! In the song "How Deep the Father's Love For Us," (by Stewart Townend), we sing, "It was *my* sin that held him there until it was accomplished. His dying breath has brought me life. I know that it is finished." I cannot sing that song without crying. His humility on the cross was not just to forgive those standing there; it was also for me, two thousand years later!

So, what are some practical ways to show gentleness and stay above all the harshness, cruelty, and anger we see around us? My farm-raised mama always told me that "you draw more flies with honey than with vinegar!" So, one important step is for us to *think about our words, our attitudes, and our actions toward others*. What do these look like in their eyes? How are they affected? Are they drawn closer, or do they want to run away? Sometimes even our "teasing" and joking can be more cruel than kind. Turn the situation around; would we want them to treat us the way we are treating them? Is there ever a justification for being thoughtless and cruel? Certainly not for a spirit-filled Christian with the fruit of gentleness! "Gracious words are like a honeycomb, sweetness to the soul and health to the body" (Proverbs 16:24, ESV).

Let's think about social media for a minute. So many people, including some Christians, say and post things they would never say in person. People behave differently on Twitter or Facebook than they do in real life. They think that they are invisible to their audience, so they feel bolder ranting and complaining about everything, not considering the consequences. That is one reason why cyberbullying has become such a huge problem, even causing some young people to commit suicide. Remember, your audience on any social medium is only one person, that one who is sitting in front of his or her personal computer or on his or her cell phone, reading your words.

It is always wise to stop and think about your posts *before posting them*! Ask yourself honestly, is this beneficial? Just because I can say it, should I? Is it true? Is it necessary? Is it kind? Are my words showing others that I honor and respect them? When they read my posts, are they drawn to the Lord by my gentleness? Remember, no one can read your tone of voice online. You may have thought you were just teasing and being funny, but others may not have understood it that way. You may feel that you have the right to say whatever you want (you know, "free speech" and all). But that is not God's way. He expects us to model his gentleness in our words as well as our actions. Ask yourself, *If I would not say this to someone in person, is it wise to say it online?*

Our Father has even more to say to us as godly women. Gentleness is a very important trait for us to model; it is what shows our true beauty to others, especially to our daughters, nieces, granddaughters, and younger sisters in Christ. "Your beauty should not come from outward adornment, such as elaborate hairstyles and the wearing of gold jewelry or fine clothes. Rather, it should be that of your inner self, the unfading beauty of a gentle and quiet spirit, which is of great worth in God's sight" (1Peter 3:3–4, NIV).

I know that sometimes we let our powerful emotions get out of control, and we say or do things we know we should not say. It might be that we have had a trying day with our little ones, or we've been on hold with the phone company for too long, or our husbands called to say they have to work late again. We let our frustrations slip out without thinking. We are not perfect. But a gentle, godly woman will realize how her words or actions have affected others and apologize quickly, seek to make amends, and gain the self-control to prevent such outbursts from happening again.

Our gentleness must go beyond our words and actions, however. As the Holy Spirit fills us more and more with his power, then our gentleness becomes a part of us inside and out. Being Spirit-filled means we are showing gentleness in our *thoughts* as well as our actions. Just because others cannot hear or see us being harsh doesn't change anything. Others may not know, but God does! The Lord told Samuel, "For the Lord sees not as man sees; man looks on the outward appearance, but the Lord looks on the heart" (1 Samuel 16:7, ESV).

Another way to improve our gentleness is to remind ourselves of God's gentleness with us. Would we really want to be on the receiving end of our own "gentleness" or lack thereof? How would we want God to correct us or point something out to us? Is it the way we do to others? Probably not. God is overwhelmingly gentle with us when we sin and need correction, and he expects us to be the same way with others.

Being gentle does not mean that we should not be strong in our beliefs, but it does imply that we should be wise and loving in expressing those beliefs to others. God sometimes shows tough love and teaches hard lessons to humans, all the while being the very definition of gentleness. "But in your hearts revere Christ as Lord. Always be prepared to give an answer to everyone who asks you to give the reason for the hope that you have. *But do this with gentleness and respect*" (1 Peter 3:15, NIV). It is always wise to err on the side of love.

As sisters in Christ, it is important for us to remember that we are all sinners, and that we are all seeking to become more like him in our words and actions. None of us is better than another. Our petty words, complaining, whining, or teasing are not really in line with godly gentleness. Our model is always Jesus. That old acronym WWJD (what would Jesus do?) really is important to remember when we are trying to show gentleness to others. It is not by our own power that gentleness becomes a part of who we are. It is only through the power of the Spirit that this will happen. Just like that old, old hymn, "Let Him Have His Way with Thee."

Let Him Have His Way with Thee

His power can make you what you ought to be;
His blood can cleanse your heart and make you free;
His love can fill your soul, and you will see
'Twas best for Him to have His way with thee.
(Cyrus Nusbaum, 1898)

So, as you work to cultivate this wonderful trait of gentleness, ask yourself these questions: Are my interactions with people marked with genuine gentleness or awkward gruffness? Do my words and body language put people at ease or put them down? Does my gentleness help to comfort, encourage, and bless?

To sum all this up, what is the best way for us to learn to be gentle? Simply spend more time with the gentle Jesus. When we are in his presence, when we truly forget about ourselves and focus on him, that brings out a softness and gentleness in us that pours out on others. In his presence, we can let all that other stuff go, rely on him, and he will make us more gentle. Troubles vanish, and hearts are mended in his presence. Then, with the Holy Spirit living in us, we can become gentle mentors to others with grace and wisdom. Our sincerity and gentleness are attractive to everyone and will draw them to our Father. Gentleness encourages gentleness in others all for God's glory. A gentle soul saves souls!

> *Grandma D.'s wisdom: I once heard someone say that no matter how old you are or how cool you may be, when a child hands you a toy phone, you always answer it! "Hello. Who is it?" That is the kind of gentleness God wants us to show others. If you think about it, we all trust our hearts to someone (it may be our family or friends—or even someone or something else). We sure hope they are gentle with us because our hearts are fragile and easily broken, aren't they? Even if someone has broken your heart, I promise you that our Father will never do so. He is always gentle and loving toward us. You can rely on him.*
>
> *Love, Grandma D.*

Chapter 11

REMOTE CONTROL OR SELF-CONTROL?

When my mom was in the last years of her life, she developed Alzheimer's. It is a cruel disease that robs someone we love of his or her life and memories, a little bit at a time. While my mom was still able to live independently, she called me several times a week because her television "wasn't working." In actuality, she was pushing buttons on the remote control and scrambling the signal until the TV would not respond. I would drive to her apartment, and she would greet me at the door, upset and frustrated, almost in tears. I would reset the remote, and she was always so grateful and apologetic. I tried to teach her how to use the remote correctly, but she was just too confused. Thankfully, she only lived a few blocks from me, so it was not a problem to go over there.

I finally came up with a solution to prevent the problem. I got some duct tape (and we all know that can solve anything!), and I covered over the buttons she was not supposed to touch. That left only the power button and channel selector open. It would make it easier for her to watch television. I thought it was the perfect solution. Sometimes, and I have no idea how, she still messed up the TV and called me to come and "fix" it again. I know you are thinking it was just an excuse to see me, but she really did mess up the signal to her television once again and was confused about how to correct it. (And honestly, I would give anything to have to fix her remote again, even one more time!)

God gives us a "remote control" for our lives, too. He knows which "buttons" or choices are safe and which ones can knock our lives out of whack. He has the directions given to us in his Word, which is his manual for living our best lives possible. Look at the earlier verses in Galatians 5, before Paul talks about the fruit of the Spirit: "Now the works of the flesh are evident: sexual immorality, impurity, sensuality, idolatry, sorcery, enmity, strife, jealousy, fits of anger, rivalries, dissensions, divisions, envy, drunkenness, orgies, and things like these. I warn you, as I warned you before, that those who do such things will not inherit the kingdom of God" (Galatians 5:19–21, ESV). That list has a lot of serious stuff on it! A lack of self-control can result in any of those works of the flesh. I look at the list and say, "Whew, I'm not tempted to do those!" Well, most of them anyway.

Our Father wants us to stay away from all those things. We have the choice to push those "buttons" or not. But God does not make our choices for us. He is not pushing buttons to run our lives his way. We are not his pets for him to train or puppets for him to control. We are people, his image-bearers, but with our own free wills. Sometimes our lack of self-control has us pushing those wrong buttons anyway—issues with our tempers, our words, our health, and so many other things. Sometimes it seems we just cannot control our human inclinations by our own wills, doesn't it? That is why God has given us the Holy Spirit to help us.

We all think we know what self-control is, but it really is still a challenge to use it in our lives! My Bible dictionary describes it as "restraint exercised over one's own impulses, emotions, or desires; to be in harmony with the will of God." Self-control is a moment-by-moment dependence on the Holy Spirit to make the right choices before us. Every day, we have countless choices to make—some simple ones like what we will wear or eat, or more challenging ones that can mean life or destruction to relationships. Self-control is literally releasing our grips on our human desires and choosing instead to be controlled by the Holy Spirit. It's a paradox—"self-less" control.

When I look at the fruit of the Spirit, I see beautiful traits—love, joy, peace, patience, kindness, goodness, faithfulness, and gentleness. But then the last one is self-control. It does not seem to fit, does it? It seems to stick out like a sore thumb! I sometimes wonder why Paul named self-control last on his list of the fruit of the Spirit. Maybe he mentioned it last because he struggled with it the most. Paul's most heart-felt confession is found in Romans 7:14–16, 18–19, 21 (NLT). Listen to the way he describes his own struggle with being "a slave to sin," his inner war with self-control:

> The trouble is not with the law, for it is spiritual and good. The trouble is with me, for I am all too human, a slave to sin. I don't really understand myself, for I want to do what is right, but I don't do it. Instead, I do what I hate … And I know that nothing good lives in me, that is, in my sinful nature. I want to do what is right, but I can't. I want to do what is good, but I don't. I don't want to do what is wrong, but I do it anyway … I have discovered this principle of life—that when I want to do what is right, I inevitably do what is wrong.

Can you hear his anguish and frustration? I imagine Paul pausing when he thinks about his wretchedness, and then with great relief and a deep sigh, he finally says, "Thanks be to God, who delivers me through Jesus Christ our Lord!" (Romans 7:25). I sure can relate to Paul's battle! Can you? If Paul, who was miraculously chosen to share God's grace with the world, can struggle with those things, I am in good company! The things I know I should do often escape me when I am faced with the temptations of pleasure and satisfaction.

Another possible reason Paul listed self-control last is that it is an important part of all the other fruitful traits, kind of like the basket that holds them all. Self-control helps us grow every one of the other traits. So, where does self-control come in? Everywhere! Here's a list a friend shared with me:

1. It takes self-control to show true godly *love* instead of lust and infatuation—to love others, not as the world loves, but as Christ loved us. "And walk in the way of love, just as Christ loved us and gave himself up for us, as a fragrant offering and sacrifice to God" (Ephesians 5:2, NIV).

2. It takes self-control to have godly *joy* when we are facing a difficult situation in life. "Though now you do not see him, yet believing, you rejoice with joy inexpressible and full of glory" (1 Peter 1:8, NKJV).

3. It takes self-control to get along with others and make *peace* instead of constantly getting into conflict. "Blessed are the peacemakers for they will be called children of God" (Matthew 5:9, NIV).

4. It takes self-control to be *patient* and bear with others rather than quickly condemning them. It is hard to "be patient with everyone" (1 Thessalonians 5:14, NIV).

5. It takes self-control to look out for the needs of others with *kindness* rather than just automatically looking out only for yourself. "In humility, value others above yourselves" (Philippians 2:4, NIV).

6. It takes self-control to do *good*, to go through the narrow gate toward life rather than the evil, wide gate that leads toward destruction (Matthew 7:13–14, ESV).

7. It takes self-control to be *faithful* and not have our faith shattered by the mocking of scoffers (2 Peter 3:3–4, ESV).

8. It takes self-control to be a *gentle* servant of the Lord (2 Timothy 2:24), showing compassion and mercy with real love as God does with us.

Honestly, when it comes to the subject of self-control, many of us would just like to ignore the issue and not talk about it. In fact, this was the one chapter I truly dreaded writing. We would like to think there is a way to put our minds, wills, and emotions under God's "remote control." Instead of having to take responsibility for our actions and decisions, we think it would be easier for God simply to control us. However, God has a more creative plan in mind. In Christ, he has given us the ability to choose right over wrong and self-control over our emotional impulses.

As Christian women, we do not see ourselves as "that bad." We do not struggle with those "major" sins. We are likely not to be tempted with immorality, drunkenness, murder, and so on. But our lists are still long ones. The temptations we face that require our self-control are just as difficult to master on our own. What about gossip, criticism, lying, bitterness, complaining, jealousy, vanity, anger, sarcasm, rationalizing, priorities, making comparisons, overeating, drinking, spending money, even time management (that includes binge-watching on Netflix), and social media? Do any of those hit a bit closer to home for you? They certainly do for me!

We have to understand that self-control and self-surrender are companions. We can quote scripture. We can count to ten. We can clench our fists and grit our teeth. We can try everything on our own to push away from temptation, but ultimately, we must surrender our weaknesses to God. I have to confess my weaknesses to him every day! *Father, I cannot do this on my own. I want to be like Jesus. I want to be guided by your Holy Spirit. Help me, please!*

Right after Jesus calmed the storm for his disciples, they stepped off the boat, and we have the story of Jesus's encounter with the demon-possessed man, whose life was definitely out of control (Mark 5). This man was filled with many evil spirits and was living among the tombs. The demons called themselves "Legion" because there were so many of them. The townspeople stayed away from the man. No one could bind him anymore, not even with chains or shackles, because he ripped the chains apart and broke the shackles in pieces. He was supernaturally strong and dangerous. This man was out of his mind, and he was destructive and terrifying. Every part of his life was filled with chaos. Jesus and his disciples were just off the boat, probably still wet, and they met the Tasmanian devil. He was spewing pure evil! I imagine the disciples were shocked. I can picture them about to panic and trying to figure out what they should do.

Now, earlier, when Jesus had calmed the storm, his disciples had asked, "Who is this that even the winds and sea obey him?" (Mark 4:41, ESV). But these demons did not ask that question; they knew who Jesus was even from a distance. Although everyone else steered clear of this terrifying man, Jesus was different. When the man saw Jesus from afar, he ran, fell down before him, and cried with a loud voice, "What have you to do with me, Jesus, Son of the Most High God? I beg you do not torment me!" (Mark 5:7, ESV). The demons knew Jesus had control over the physical world (the wind, the waves, and the storm), as well as the spiritual realm. They begged him to send them into a nearby herd of pigs. This was a very large herd of over two thousand pigs! Cool, calm, in-control Jesus gave them permission with just a word. The demons entered the herd of now loud, squealing pigs. They madly ran off the cliff and drowned in the water below.

What about the man? That once wild, dangerous, tormented man was quietly sitting there in his right mind. Within just a few minutes, he went from having no idea about a loving God to being instantly freed in every way. This same man suddenly became emotionally stable and physically at peace. He had full control of his mind and body.

You see, the one who calms the storms in the physical world can also calm the storms within us. We also have been set free from the bondage of sin. He may not calm all my storms, but he can calm me. I may not always make the wisest decisions. I may still have struggles, but I know I am getting a little bit closer to his will with each right choice I make.

Having self-control can be challenging if we take our focus off God's will and purpose for us. It can affect our minds, our bodies, and our emotions. It is only with the help of the Holy Spirit that we can gain self-control over each of these.

First, it is only with the Spirit's help that we can have *self-control over our minds*. When you are thinking, what are you thinking about? What thoughts consume your mind? We have been blessed with an amazing brain to imagine, create, and think. Sadly, we spend more time "not thinking," but instead sifting through junk on television or the internet, especially on social media. Yes, we can become prisoners to our cell phones, can't we? Believe me, I'm guilty, too.

Some of us struggle and are overwhelmed with feelings that want to spiral out of control. There is a common pattern—our emotions lead to our thoughts, our thoughts affect our decisions, and our decisions determine our behaviors. Those behaviors can cause a positive or negative impact on our relationships. Not only can they affect our relationships with our families, our friends, or our coworkers, but they can also have an impact on our relationships with God. It sounds pretty hopeless, doesn't it?

The apostle Paul had a simple answer, "Take every thought captive to obey Christ" (2 Corinthians 10:5, ESV). It sounds impossible. Can we really take every thought captive? I know my thoughts sometimes seem to be out of control and running two steps ahead of me!

God knows that it really is possible to have control over our thoughts. But how? First, we need to recognize that not all thoughts that pop into our heads are true; the lies we "listen to" in our heads are not from God! For example, If I tell myself that I am a failure, that is Satan trying to weaken my faith and question my value, I know that God would never tell me that! He knows I am not a failure. It is up to me to kick those thoughts to the door. Sometimes I have to say out loud, "Satan, leave me alone!"

Of course, we must replace those negative thoughts with godly ones. There are many passages in the Bible that can fill us with God's positive messages. Here are two of my favorites that I have recited in my head many times: "I can do all things through him who gives me strength" (Philippians 4:13, NIV), and "In all these things we are more than conquerors through him who loved us" (Romans 8:37, ESV).

When we replace negative thoughts with positive God-centered thoughts, we can gain self-control over our minds. It is not always an easy process if your mind has been filled with pain and negativity for a long time, but it can be done. I do not ever want to make light of depression or anxiety. They can be very consuming. You may need to find a Christian counselor or friend who can help you see the value in changing your focus to positive thoughts. God wants you to be confident in your value and worth. He loves you no matter what, but he knows that your thoughts can defeat you.

Next, it is the Spirit who shows us how to gain *self-control over our bodies*. When God created us, he formed our bodies and breathed our spirits into us. We became people who reflect the image of God. Then God became human and took on a body like ours, so actually we reflect the image of God both physically and spiritually (1 Corinthians 6:2).

Temptations are not new to us. Jesus understood hunger and was tempted to eat bread instead of honoring God with his body. Your body is a temple. You are exceptional. Taking good care of your body honors God. Whether you struggle with overeating or under-exercising, you can find ways to honor the Spirit that lives within you. (Actually, I am preaching to myself here!) Self-control over my eating choices is one of my areas of weakness. I could have a PhD in weight loss and healthy eating. I know what to do; I know what foods I should eat, but sometimes those chips and queso keep calling my name! (I mean, I live in Texas. You have to love chips and queso! It's in the state bylaws or something.)

Or then there are the peanut M&Ms my husband keeps buying in those jumbo-size jars at Sam's Club! They taste so good. They are creamy, crunchy, chocolatey, and salty altogether, and all those pretty colors … oh my! Now I know that occasionally I could safely eat a small amount, and that would be okay. But for me, a "small amount" can be such a relative term! I know that once I start, my willpower disappears. Seriously, I finally told my husband to hide those evil M&Ms because I just wanted to eat all of them at one time. He sweetly said, "Just don't do it. Have a little willpower." It took all my self-control not to dump them on his head!

Finally, we can also glorify God by gaining *self-control over our emotions*. We know that we are called to show love to others just as Jesus has shown love to us. But we women are more emotional than men. Okay, I said it. Don't bop me on the head; we know that it's true. God made us that way so we could show greater empathy and compassion for others. We hurt when they hurt, and that makes us more caring and responsive to their needs. Emotions can be a good thing, but we women tend to make excuses for our emotions. We can blame our spouses, our children, our friends, even "that time of the month."

Sometimes it is anger that gets control of us. Anger in and of itself is not the problem, but how we show it is! Do you yell, throw things, or say things you regret? Or maybe you give someone the silent treatment, holding it all inside. Anger can lead to so many other negative emotions—jealousy, negativity, selfishness, bitterness, hate—which can all destroy our relationships.

Our emotions are our choices. We are supposed to be controlling them, not letting them control us. And as I mentioned previously, we must replace the negative with the positive. When you allow the Holy Spirit to fill you with peace, joy, and gentleness, those negative emotions will not run rampant, and you will not feel out of control. I hate that feeling!

As a woman of God, I know the struggles I have with self-control over my mind, over my body, and over my emotions. When I am feeling stressed, angry, tired, frustrated, or hurt, I know God wants to calm those storms within me. That is the best time for me to stop and pray. Sometimes I turn on some Christian music and sing. Other times, I go for a walk, take a bath, or call a friend who can help me stop that cycle of negative emotions and wrong choices. However, it is best for me to have a plan in place before I let stress and negativity get to me.

God knows how much we want to feel in control of our lives. He also knows that we want more than anything to please him. Be patient with yourself. If you mess up, fess up and try again. As we grow more into the image of Christ, it will become easier to allow the mind of Christ to help us make our decisions. When we demonstrate self-control, we are really announcing that the Savior is in control within us. He is the ruler of our minds, our bodies, and our emotions. If the Son sets you free, you are free indeed, in every way, every day. And that feels mighty good!

> *Grandma D.'s wisdom: I wish self-control was easy, don't you? I would be skinny and always do and say the right things. But then, I wouldn't need a Savior, would I? The older I get, the more I know I need Spirit-control before I can ever really have self-control. How about you? Are you willing to let him have his way with your life? It really does get easier. I promise.*
>
> *Love, Grandma D.*

Chapter 12

HANGING ON
(CONFESSIONS OF A
FLIMSY BRANCH)

Have you noticed that people like to say that forty is the new thirty, sixty is the new forty, or whatever age is "younger" than the calendar shows? Now that I am older, I understand why they say that. For one thing, our society is aging. The baby boomer generation is getting up there in years, but we don't *feel* old. The inside of a person doesn't always match what the outside looks like. Those sayings help us old folks to not really feel so ancient!

Even though I feel younger on the inside, I know I have lived quite a few years. Thankfully, during those years I have experienced the influence of the Holy Spirit in my life more times than I can count. So, you would think that I could finally say, *Now I get it!* But I still feel like I know less than a grain of sand on a long beach! Why do I still forget how powerful he is? Why do I keep trying to do life on my own? Unbelievable, isn't it?

The Holy Spirit *is* God! He was there along with the Father and Jesus when the world was created, and time began. He gave wisdom and guidance to the prophets and spiritual leaders throughout the Old Testament. He was with Jesus throughout his years on earth, helping him during his ministry and comforting him as he faced death on the cross.

When Jesus was about to go back to heaven, he knew his followers would need that same kind of comforter as well. The Holy Spirit came not to just be with them, but to live inside them.

As we talked about in chapter 2, we have access to that same Holy Spirit. You see, Jesus's death on the cross gave us the opportunity to become part of God's family. He won't force us; it's our choice whether or not to receive this gift. When we choose to become his children, we "die" to our own selfish wills. We are made clean with all our sins washed away—never to be brought up again or ever to have our noses rubbed in them. Now we walk in a new kind of life and receive the gift of the Holy Spirit within us as well. What an amazing gift he is, too! He is our leader, guide, teacher, and comforter. His presence in us means that we are God's children, and that God has upheld his promise to always be with us.

After Jesus celebrated his last Passover with his disciples, they left the upper room and went for a walk. Judas had already left to betray him, so it was just Jesus and the eleven others. Maybe they were going to the temple. Or maybe, as I would imagine it, they were taking a slow stroll on the quiet streets of Jerusalem, heading out of the city to the garden of Gethsemane.

Jesus knew that he had only a few hours left to be with them. He still had so much he wanted to tell them. His disciples had no idea where they were heading and no clue what was going to happen there. I'm sure those men had so many questions—why did Jesus tell us to remember him when he's right here? Where is he going that we can't go? Where did Judas go in such a hurry? Why is Jesus so sad?

All Jesus wanted to do was to spend as much time as he could with these men he dearly loved. His heart was so heavy knowing that, in just a few hours, he would be arrested, and they would be scared and confused. But even more than he worried about the pain he would soon suffer, he was concerned about them. He knew they would all desert him, but he also knew they would later suffer so much, even death, for his name.

As they walked, I imagine they passed several vineyards, as the area was filled with them. It was springtime, so the leaves were green, but the luscious grapes were only just peeking out of the buds. He paused, put his hand on a strong, twisted vine, and told them something surprising.

"I am the true vine," he said. "And my Father is the vinedresser" (John 15:1, ESV). That was quite a statement. All they had ever heard was that the children of Israel were called God's vine.

Throughout the Old Testament, the Israelites repeatedly turned their backs on God and worshipped idols. In Isaiah 5:1–7 (NIV), God talked about how much he loved them and how he had cared for them as a vinedresser does for his precious vineyard. Then he asked, "What more could have been done for my vineyard than I have done for it? When I looked for good grapes, why did it yield only bad?" (verse four). Those wild grapes were sour and not good for anything. They just had to be thrown away or made into vinegar.

Even with all of God's love and care, the children of Israel did what they pleased and were not faithful to him. So in that same passage, God said, "Now I will tell you what I am going to do to my vineyard. I will take away its hedge, and it will be destroyed; I will break down it's wall [protection], and it will be trampled. I will make it a wasteland, neither pruned nor cultivated, and briers and thorns will grow there …" (verses five and six). And that is just what happened.

God allowed Israel to be captured by Babylon. The Babylonian king, Nebuchadnezzar, destroyed the city, including the temple. The Israelites were no longer the chosen vine. They were just helpless, enslaved people without their home and without their God. The only hope they had left was for the promised Messiah to come. In the four hundred or so years between the Old Testament and the New Testament, Judah was ruled by first the Greeks, then the Syrians, and then the Romans. (I'm sure you've heard of Julius Caesar, right?)

So, in John 15, Jesus had just told his disciples that he was that true vine—the Messiah. He also added that his father was the vinedresser. Of course, his disciples didn't understand exactly what he meant. They were still expecting him to conquer the world and make himself the earthly king.

Jesus talked not only about his role as the vine and his Father as the vinedresser, but about the responsibilities of his followers as the fruit-bearing branches. The words Jesus shared with his disciples are just as relevant for us today. Bearing fruit is part of our job description, and there are rewards when we do it right and consequences when we don't.

I love the imagery in John 15, and I have read many articles about vineyards. It is a fascinating process from vine to wine. But there is so much to learn and understand! Being a vinedresser—or vintner, as they are called today—is a complicated job, a combination of science and art. It takes the vintner knowing his vines and constantly watching over them for them to bear the sweetest, healthiest grapes. So, before we can better understand Jesus's allegory in John 15, let's look at what it takes for vines and branches to make grapes.

I realized that for me to get a clearer picture of how a vineyard works, I needed to visit one. I live in North Texas, and there are a few vineyards not too far from me. (We even have a town nearby called Grapevine.) I discovered a lovely family-owned vineyard in Celina, Texas, called Eden Hill. I was so blessed to visit with the owner and operations manager, Clark Hornbaker, and his office manager, Sheri Richter. What a treat it was to spend time with them. I learned so much, not only about the operation of the vineyard and winery, but also about the heart and passion of the vintner as he cares for the vines and grapes. I must admit that my head was spinning a bit with all the science and skills needed for a successful harvest.

Eden Hill was founded in 2007. The amazing thing about vineyards is that it takes four years just to see the first crops. That means the vintner has to have a lot of patience and faith that all his hard work now will be rewarded with sweet grapes later. Grapevines are not what we think about when we picture vines. They are not like ivy that winds its way around a tree or up the side of a building. Grapevines are thick, gnarly trunks, some several inches in diameter, that connect the roots to the branches.

A few feet above the ground (about three to four feet high), the vines are trained to grow horizontally in either direction. They are usually tied or wrapped around a wire that is part of a trellis. These parts of the vine are called cordons. It is from these cordons that the shoots, or branches, grow upward, several on either side. There are always too many shoots that grow too close to each other. They won't produce a bounty of healthy grapes, so most of the shoots must be cut off even if they are growing well. This leaves enough room between the remaining shoots for large clusters to grow.

As warm temperatures arrive in spring, little green buds begin to form on the shoots. The buds will soon flower, and tiny grapes will appear. The vines continually carry nourishment and water from the soil to the branches and the growing fruit. According to Clark, there are many responsibilities the vintner has in each season of the year. He always watches and gets to know every vine and its branches. Each one has different needs depending on its location in the vineyard, the nutrients in the soil, the strength and health of the branches, the "critters" and pests that come along, the quality of grape clusters they have produced in the past, and the amount of pruning they will need to be even more fruitful in the future. That is so much to consider when caring for those vines!

Pruning is, by far, Clark's toughest job. Cutting away dead shoots or unfruitful branches is obvious because they are not benefiting the vine. What is more difficult is pruning those branches that are strong and growing. As we walked through the vineyard, Clark pointed out branches that looked perfectly healthy, but that he would need to cut off when the plants go dormant. This process will train the branches to grow more efficiently. He explained that if he doesn't cut some of the hearty ones back, there will be smaller grape clusters the next season, and even in future seasons after that. He knows that each careful snip of his shears will have an effect on the next season and many seasons to come.

As the vintner trains the grapevines, they will produce the right amount of fruit. So many factors—the pruning, training, fertilizing, watering, and the weather—work together to create just the right balance that is needed for the best harvest. If mistakes are made, the grapevines are out of balance, and there can be long-term consequences. I asked Clark if he had ever made a mistake. Yes, he has made mistakes over the years. He assured me that the vines are forgiving; it just takes them three years to do so!

As Jesus and his disciples continued their walk to Gethsemane, he talked more about God as the vinedresser and his care for the vine and the branches. Did they really understand his allegory was referring to those who are in the kingdom of God and those who are not? I don't know. Maybe they did, but my guess is that they probably didn't fully understand until after Jesus had left them and they received the Holy Spirit. Then they would see for themselves his power in their lives and the fruit they would produce with his help.

Jesus assured his disciples that the vinedresser always keeps a watchful eye on his vineyard. As he surveys each branch, he looks for fruit growing from them. Then he will do one of two things—he will take away fruitless branches and prune fruitful ones. He cuts away the lifeless, and he cultivates the living. In fact, if you notice, God does not leave any branch unattended.

Jesus said that the branches that don't produce fruit will be cut off and thrown in the fire. You see, they understood that dead grapevine branches were basically useless. The wood is not even strong enough to make furniture. It can be used for only one thing—kindling in a fire. That is the same fate that God says awaits those who are not connected to the true vine, Jesus Christ.

For those of us who try to bear fruit in our lives, our vinedresser wants more. He knows that each of us is unique with our own strengths and weaknesses. Just like a vintner at Eden Hill, our Father knows that careful pruning will help us to produce the sweetest and most abundant fruit. He doesn't just hack away at us; he gently prunes just the right amount for us to grow. For some of us, it may mean only a snip here and there. But for others, he may cut off some serious dead wood—maybe this is something or someone preventing us from being what he wants us to be. To our human eyes, it could be something that seems perfectly healthy and fine to us. We have to trust that he knows better than we do.

Sometimes, he may prune us in other ways. For example, he might allow trials to come into our lives so we will learn to trust him. Whatever the reason, pruning really hurts! We don't always understand or like the process, but we have to believe that our heavenly Father loves us and has our best interests at heart. Sometimes when we face challenging circumstances, we think we have to figure it all out on our own, but in reality, all we really need to do is trust our vinedresser, the one knows us best. He is on our side. That's what matters most on those hard, pruning days. That's what gives us sweet rewards.

So, what is the difference between those who produce fruit and those who don't? It is all tied to one word—*abide*. What does abide mean? It means to stay, to remain, or to live in him. There are benefits of abiding that we cannot have on our own. In John 15:4–5 (ESV), Jesus explains, "Abide in me, and I in you. As the branch cannot bear fruit by itself, unless it abides in the vine, neither can you, unless you abide in me. I am the vine; you are the branches. Whoever abides in me and I in him, he it is that bears much fruit, for apart from me you can do nothing." So by abiding, we have his strength within us, and his love is manifested in our lives.

There are even more special benefits of abiding in him. In John 15:7 (NIV), he said, "If you remain in me and my words remain in you, ask whatever you wish, and it will be done for you." That is a big promise! It doesn't mean you are a little girl asking Daddy to give you a pony. When you abide in him, your deepest desire is to please him in all you do. That means whatever you ask for, he will give it to you because you will ask for the right things for the right reasons. So staying connected to Jesus, our heavenly vine, is vital for us to remain healthy and growing. Our goal is to grow more and more into his image. If we don't abide, then we are not connected to Jesus. We are just like flimsy sticks stuck randomly in the ground. Nothing can come from unconnected, rootless sticks!

One of the most fascinating things about grape production is how there are so many factors throughout the year that affect the grapevines and how they will produce a sweet, bountiful harvest. Again, the wise vintner knows just what to do for this to happen. In the summertime when the grapes are ripening on the vine, it is time for canopy management. The canopy is a protection for the grapes; it is actually the perfect number of leaves that provide just the right balance of sunlight and shade for the grapes to ripen fully. The canopy protects the fruit from strong winds and excessive summer heat. Clark calls this process "magical," as it is the sun that causes photosynthesis in the vine and leaves. Keeping this at just the right balance is how the sun produces the perfect amount of sugar and sweetness in the grapes.

The wise vintner will regularly go through the vineyard to check each plant, pulling off leaves to keep the sunlight shining on the grape clusters. If the vintner pulls off too many leaves, the grapes will ripen too fast, which can cause them to turn brown and shrivel up. Not enough sunlight will impede the growth of the grapes and can even cause grape diseases. This will prevent photosynthesis from creating that magical sweetness that the vintner wants in his wine.

With all his years of practice and understanding the needs of each plant, Clark knows just the right number of leaves to make the perfect canopy over each cluster of grapes. That isn't something he learned from a book; it is truly from someone who knows and cares about his vineyard!

Isn't that also true for us? When the Son of God is shining on our hearts, our sweetness grows. Sometimes we allow other things to block his "son-light" in our lives. It could be major problems—health issues, family struggles, or financial strains. It could also be those everyday worries and concerns that we women sometimes hold on to—hurt feelings, stress, low self-esteem, fatigue, and even hormones. When we focus on these things, we block out the sweet joy and contentment that are found only in him. Thankfully, just like in the vineyard, our Savior never leaves us alone. He provides his perfect protection, and all we have to do is abide in him.

Even in the dormant season, late fall and winter, when the plants appear to be "sleeping," many actions are still happening under the surface. The roots are still growing and creating sap that will travel up the vine in early spring to provide nourishment and protection even before the grapes blossom. It is an amazing process that God himself designed when he first created plants and trees when he was making the world.

Walking through the vineyard at Eden Hill was a peaceful, almost holy experience. I marveled as I touched those rough vines, the twisted cordons, and the stately leaves that would soon change colors and fall to the ground. God's presence was there. As I learned about all those steps just to have sweet grapes, I couldn't wait to see the harvest they would yield. Clark invited me to come back and help pick those grapes when the time was perfect. Harvest is the reward for his dedication and faithfulness.

Several months later, I had the pleasure to be part of a crew to harvest those beautiful grapes. It was a smaller harvest in 2021 because of the unusually cold winter in Texas as well as some unexpected animals that had helped themselves to the fruit. Clark showed me how to cut the grape clusters and to watch for mold or other damage. We smelled the sweetness of ripe grapes and compared that with the bitterness of those that had spoiled. It was a fun task, lifting those large green leaves to discover plump, deep purple clusters hiding below them. With a snip here and there, the grapes were gently put into crates and then taken by a tractor to the winery.

Chris Hornbaker, Clark's son, is their chief winemaker. It was his expertise that determined the exact day and time for the harvesting. He oversees each of the steps for making their perfect wine—getting the grapes from the vineyard to the winery, then the process of inspecting, cleaning, and mashing the grapes (which isn't done by stomping them with your feet like Lucille Ball did in *I Love Lucy*). Next, the new wine, which is still not drinkable, is put into stainless steel tanks where it will stay and sweeten for about two years or more. When Chris tastes that it is at just the right sweetness, the wine is bottled, labeled, and shipped to stores and customers around the world. (Of course, it's quite a bit more complicated and scientific than that. But it is a fascinating process.)

I'm so thankful that God has a plan for a bountiful harvest in my life and yours as well. He gives us abundant blessings every day. His fruit makes our lives have the perfect sweetness, too.

Several years ago, while growing my first backyard vegetable garden, I decided to make a compost pile as well. Pretty industrious, wouldn't you say? My husband nailed some boards together, and I regularly threw in all the leftover "garbage"—vegetable scraps, banana peels, eggshells, coffee grounds, grass clippings, and anything else I could think of—into that pile. It sure wasn't pretty and was quite a contrast from the budding garden. But as all that waste decomposed, I knew it was going to make the richest soil that I would use in my future gardens.

By the next spring, I was excited about planting a bigger garden and expanding it with peppers, beans, watermelons, and cantaloupes. As I started to move some of that rich soil from the compost pile into the garden, I noticed that not only was the garden sprouting, but the compost pile was as well! One little green plant was pushing up through the soil and remaining waste. I was surprised and a bit curious, so I decided to just leave it alone.

Before too long, I noticed a vine with leaves that looked a lot like my zucchini plants growing nearby. It continued to grow, and I actually got two yummy zucchinis from that plant. And my family loved eating those delicious zucchinis sautéed with some of my lovely garden tomatoes. It is hard to believe that something beautiful came from that garbage pile!

That's what God did for us, too. He took all our messes, all our sins, all our garbage, and nailed them to the cross. We were made new and beautiful, transformed into the image of Christ. I am so glad that I am not measured by my mistakes, my problems, and my junk. Neither are you! He wants to grow something wonderful in the compost of your life. You just have to let the Holy Spirit do his business in your heart. That's how the fruit will come.

So, now we are in the final chapter of this book. We have looked at the nine traits of the Holy Spirit's fruit living in us, the traits we model when we yield to his will. Our fruitful lives model his spiritual traits, not ours. It is his love, joy, peace, patience, kindness, goodness, faithfulness, and self-control that the world will see in us and want to know more about our heavenly Father.

I must confess—sometimes I try to model these traits on my own strength. Sometimes I try to let others think I have it all together. Guess what? Even at my age, I don't! And even if I did have it "all together," I would be concerned about who I was truly depending on! It all goes back to the fact that Jesus is the vine, and I am not. I am just a weak, flimsy branch that cannot manage life on my own. But I really don't want to. God's plans for my life are much richer and more satisfying than my plans ever could be. It's his recipe of divine fruit that I know will make my life more peaceful, joyful, and fulfilling. I may not always feel worthy, but Jesus's death makes me worthy. And because of him, I will be more fruitful as well.

My prayer for you, my dear book buddy, is that you can live confidently knowing that he has you in his hand and will never let you go (Psalm 139:10). He hears even the unspoken prayers of your heart. In fact, he tunes out all the noisy chaos of the world and leans his ear just to hear your prayers (Psalm 116:2). Your name is engraved on his palm (Isaiah 49:16), and there is no way he will ever forget you. He has always held the universe and our little parts of it in his hands. You cannot lose with him. You cannot be overcome, so go and be fruity!

> *Grandma D.'s wisdom: I love that word* abide. *Did you know another definition of it is to rest? As we stay in him, trusting and resting in his loving care, we can relax knowing that he will make everything work out for our good, no matter what! I hope you can feel his love for you, my sweet friend. You are precious in his sight. Never forget that. You are connected to the holy vine of God, and he will never let you go.*
>
> *Love, Grandma D.*

Study Questions

Chapter 1 – *The Potluck*

1. Read Galatians 5:22-23. Which fruit of the Spirit traits are easier for you to model in your life? Why do you think they are easy?

_____

_____

_____

2. Now the harder part – which fruit do you struggle with? Why are they difficult for you?

_____

_____

_____

3. How can the Holy Spirit help you to grow fruit in your life?

_____

_____

_____

Chapter 2 – *Not by Might, Not by Power*

1. The title of this chapter comes from Zechariah 4:6. Why are might and power useless in our battle against the enemy?

   _____

   _____

   _____

2. In what ways can the Holy Spirit help you in your daily life? How can you know he is working?

   _____

   _____

   _____

3. Why is it important for the Holy Spirit to intercede in your prayer life?

   _____

   _____

   _____

Chapter 3 – *Love. Period.*

1. What is a covenant? Why is it an important aspect of your relationship with God?

   _____

   _____

   _____

2. What are the important traits of God's love for his children? Which means most to you?

_____

_____

_____

3. Of the four Greek words for love, agape is the most God-like. What are some ways you can show agape to others?

_____

_____

_____

Chapter 4 – *Joy, Joy, Joy, Joy Down in My Heart*

1. What is the difference between joy and happiness?

_____

_____

_____

2. Why do you think Jesus counted his death on the cross as "pure joy?"

_____

_____

_____

3. How can you be joyful in struggles, trials, or even in pain?

_____

_____

_____

Chapter 5 – *A Piece of Peace*

1. Read John 14:27. How is worldly peace different from godly peace?

_____

_____

_____

2. What are some ways that worry can rob you of your peace? How can you prevent this?

_____

_____

_____

3. How can your sins and guilt rob you of peace? What lies does Satan tell you?

_____

_____

_____

Chapter 6 – *Annoying an Oyster*

1. Why is it so difficult to be patient? Why do some translations call it longsuffering?

   _____

   _____

   _____

2. How does your impatience affect those around you? How can you model patience when feeling stressed?

   _____

   _____

   _____

3. What practical steps can you take to stop impatient thoughts before they become actions?

   _____

   _____

   _____

Chapter 7 – *A Net of Kindness*

1. What are some of the many ways God shows kindness to his children? To the world?

   _____

   _____

   _____

2. How have others shown kindness to you? How did that make you feel?

_____

_____

_____

3. What are some practical ways you can show kindness to others – both those you know as well as strangers?

_____

_____

_____

Chapter 8 – *Goodness Gracious!*

1. Why is God called "good?" What has he done to show you his goodness?

_____

_____

_____

2. What is the difference between goodness and kindness? Give an example.

_____

_____

_____

3. Godly goodness goes beyond the moment. How can you show this goodness to others?

_____

_____

_____

Chapter 9 – *Faithful in the Fire*

1. What words describe God's faithfulness toward his children?

_____

_____

_____

2. Which promises of God remind you of his faithfulness in your life?

_____

_____

_____

3. This chapter is called "Faithful in the Fire." What are some fires God has brought you through? How were you able to trust him?

_____

_____

_____

Chapter 10 – *Gentle as a Chicken*

1. How does the world see gentleness? How does God see it?

_____

_____

_____

2. What ways can you make your gentleness visible to others?

_____

_____

_____

3. How important is your gentleness when you post comments online? Why?

_____

_____

_____

Chapter 11 – *Remote Control of Self-Control?*

1. Why do you think self-control is so difficult to master? What do you struggle with most?

_____

_____

_____

2. How do you get control over your thoughts? Your body? Your emotions?

_____

_____

_____

3. How is self-control connected with self-surrender?

_____

_____

_____

Chapter 12 – *Hanging On (Confessions of a Flimsy Branch)*

1. What does God do to the unfruitful branches in his vineyard? How does he care for the fruitful ones?

_____

_____

_____

2. In what ways has God pruned your life? What was the result?

_____

_____

_____

3. What does it mean to "abide" in Jesus, the vine? What are the benefits to abiding in him?

_____

_____

_____

Appendix

As I mentioned in Chapter 3, God's love for us is perfect. He created each of us with such tenderness and care. He knew everything about us even before we took our first breaths. Here is that beautiful passage.

PSALM 139

O Lord, you have searched me and known me! You know when I sit down and when I rise up; you discern my thoughts from afar. You search out my path and my lying down and are acquainted with all my ways. Even before a word is on my tongue, behold, O Lord, you know it altogether. You hem me in, behind and before, and lay your hand upon me. Such knowledge is too wonderful for me; it is high; I cannot attain it.

Where shall I go from your Spirit? Or where shall I flee from your presence? If I ascend to heaven, you are there! If I make my bed in Sheol, you are there! If I take the wings of the morning and dwell in the uttermost parts of the sea, even there your hand shall lead me, and your right hand shall hold me. If I say, "Surely the darkness shall cover me, and the light about me be night," even the darkness is not dark to you; the night is bright as the day, for darkness is as light with you. For you formed my inward parts; you knitted me together in my mother's womb, I praise you, for I am fearfully and wonderfully made. Wonderful are your works; my soul knows it very well. My frame was not hidden from you, when I was being made in secret, intricately woven in the depths of the earth. Your eyes saw my unformed substance; in your book were written, every one of them, the days that were formed for me, when as yet there was none of them.

How precious to me are your thoughts, O God! How vast is the sum of them! If I would count them, they are more than the sand. I awake, and I am still with you. Oh that you would slay the wicked, O God! O men of blood, depart from me! They speak against you with malicious intent; your enemies take your name in vain! Do I not hate those who hate you, O Lord? And do I not loathe those who rise up against you? I hate them with complete hatred; I count them my enemies. Search me, O God, and know my heart! Try me and know my thoughts! And see if there be any grievous way in me and lead me in the way everlasting!

About the Author

Diana Kinser is an author, blogger (www.Grandma-D.com), retired educator, Bible teacher, public speaker, painter, mother, and grandmother. She earned a bachelor's degree in journalism from Abilene Christian University and her teaching certification from Texas Women's University. Kinser is a former newspaper journalist and editor; a television writer and reporter; freelance book editor; and script and media writer for a Christian television program. She lives in Aubrey, Texas, with her husband, Clay, and their two miniature schnauzers.

Printed in the United States
by Baker & Taylor Publisher Services